CW00499825

T H E   B O O K   O F

VEGETARIAN
COOKING

T H E   B O O K   O F

VEGETARIAN
COOKING

LOUISE PICKFORD

Photographed by
JON STEWART

a Salamander book

Published by Salamander Books Limited
LONDON • NEW YORK

Published 1993 by Salamander Books Limited
129-137 York Way, London N7 9LG, United Kingdom

© Salamander Books Ltd 1993

ISBN 0-86101-748-X

Distributed by Hodder & Stoughton Services, PO Box 6,
Mill Road, Dunton Green, Sevenoaks, Kent TN13 2XX

Managing Editor: Felicity Jackson
Art Director: Roger Daniels
Editor: Louise Steele
Photographer: Jon Stewart, assisted by Nicole Mai
Home Economists: Kerenza Harries and Jo Craig
Typeset by: BMD Graphics, Hemel Hempstead
Colour separation by: Scantrans Pte. Ltd, Singapore
Printed in Belgium by Proost International Book Production

ACKNOWLEDGEMENTS

The Publishers would like to thank the following for their
help and advice:
Barbara Stewart at Prop Exchange, Unit F,
51 Calthorpe Street, London WC1.

Notes:
All spoon measurements are equal.
1 teaspoon = 5 ml spoon
1 tablespoon = 15 ml spoon.

CONTENTS

INTRODUCTION

With the emphasis on a more healthy lifestyle, vegetarian cooking is fast becoming the most attractive way of providing a highly nutritious and versatile diet. *The Book of Vegetarian Cooking* is a delicious collection of recipes based on unusual combinations of fresh vegetables, fruits, pasta, rice, grains, eggs and cheeses, with recipes for both vegetarians and vegans, as well as those who simply enjoy meatless dishes.

Low-fat alternatives to cream and cheese are given in many of the recipes, and butter is only suggested where it is essential for the flavour of the dish. However, there are some rich and creamy dishes for those who enjoy the occasional indulgence.

The recipes are drawn from all parts of the world to give a truly international selection. Divided into nine chapters, this book offers a wide choice of recipes, ranging from warming winter soups and elegant starters, light brunches and suppers, and sensational salads, to elegant dinner party dishes and wickedly indulgent puddings.

With over 100 recipes, each one illustrated in full colour and with step-by-step instructions, this is the essential book for vegetarians who want to enjoy a varied diet. By planning your meals from the recipes in this book, you will be able to ensure a well-balanced and healthy diet, with food that is fun to cook and delicious to eat.

THE VEGETARIAN DIET

A well-balanced diet is essential for healthy living. It is generally accepted that we should all eat less fat, sugar and salt and more cereals, starchy foods, vitamins and minerals. By excluding meat in your diet, you can decrease your fat intake, but do not replace meat with too much high-fat dairy produce, with the misguided notion you are only replacing lost protein.

Many staple foods such as nuts, breads, soya products and brown rice all contain high proportions of protein. Essential minerals and vitamins are present in many fresh vegetables, and by eating starchy foods, particularly rice, pasta and bread, you can get a good supply of complex carbohydrates.

The following are some of the ingredients used that may be unfamiliar.

Balsamic vinegar: an Italian vinegar aged in barrels. It is dark in colour with a slightly sweet flavour.

Creamed coconut: sold in blocks, this flavours and thickens sauces, but it should only be used in small amounts. It will curdle if allowed to boil.

Crème fraîche: a thick cream similar to sour cream, which will not curdle when cooked at a high temperature.

Dried ceps: dried mushrooms also known as porcini; these have an intense flavour and are used in small amounts. Reconstitute in boiling water before using.

Grated horseradish: freshly grated horseradish is available in jars. Alternatively, use creamed horseradish.

Kirsch: a cherry flavoured liqueur.

Lemon grass: a hard grass used in Far Eastern cooking, this has a fragrant lemon flavour and should be lightly crushed to allow flavours to escape. Available from ethnic stores.

Mascarpone: an Italian fresh cream cheese, with a light texture and natural sweet flavour.

Mushrooms: when a recipe calls for mixed mushrooms, use any different fresh varieties available, such as field, ceps, oyster and shiitake.

Pecorino: an Italian semi-hard cheese with a flavour similar to Parmesan.

Polenta: a coarse grained cornmeal.

Puy lentils: small blue-brown lentils, with a delicious nutty flavour; brown or green lentils may be used instead.

Sechuan pepper: highly aromatic reddish-brown peppercorns used in Oriental cooking

Sun-dried tomatoes: dried tomatoes which are sold either in packets and need to be reconstituted in boiling water, or in oil, when they simply need to be drained. They have an intensely sweet tomato flavour, and should only be used in small quantities. Sun-dried tomato paste is also available.

Tamarind paste: made from the bean-like fruit of the tamarind tree, the paste has a lemony flavour.

OTHER INGREDIENTS

Butter should be unsalted wherever possible; substitute vegetable margarine or oil, if wished.

Vegetable stock should be home-made if possible; see the recipe on page 65, or blend good-quality stock cubes with vegetable cooking water.

Olive oil, if used raw, should always be Virgin. A lesser quality oil can be used for frying, grilling and roasting.

Sea salt should be used when possible, and pepper should always be freshly ground black peppercorns unless otherwise stated.

HIDDEN DANGERS

Strict vegetarians should be careful to check packets before purchasing products. The foods that may contain animal products are cheeses – many of the recipes state a particular vegetarian cheese or suggest alternatives – wines and bottled sauces.

ITALIAN BEAN SOUP

175 g (6 oz/1 cup) dried borlotti beans,
 soaked overnight in cold water to cover
1 bay leaf
1 sprig each thyme and rosemary
1.2 litres (40 fl oz/5 cups) vegetable stock
2 tablespoons olive oil
1 onion, chopped
1 clove garlic, chopped
1 teaspoon each chopped fresh rosemary,
 sage and thyme
2 carrots, chopped
2 sticks celery, chopped
1 large courgette (zucchini), chopped
85 ml (3 fl oz/⅓ cup) red wine
300 ml (10 fl oz/1¼ cups) tomato juice
2 tablespoons chopped fresh parsley

Drain the beans and place in a large pan with
the bay leaf, thyme and rosemary sprigs. Add
the stock, bring to the boil and boil for 10
minutes. Reduce heat, cover and cook gently
for 45-50 minutes until beans are cooked.
Heat the oil and fry the onion, garlic, chopped rosemary, sage and thyme, carrots, celery
and courgette (zucchini) for 5 minutes. Add
the wine and boil rapidly for 3 minutes. Add
the tomato juice, cover and simmer gently for
20 minutes.

Strain the cooked beans, reserving the stock.
Purée half the beans in a blender or food
processor with 150 ml (5 fl oz/⅔ cup) of the
stock and stir into the tomato and vegetable
mixture. Stir in the remaining beans, 850 ml
(30 fl oz/3¾ cups) stock, parsley and salt and
pepper. Bring to the boil and cook for a
further 5 minutes.

Serves 8.

- MUSHROOM & BARLEY BROTH -

85 g (3 oz/⅓ cup) pot barley, soaked overnight in cold
    water to cover
1 litre (35 fl oz/4½ cups) vegetable stock
15 g (½ oz/¼ cup) dried ceps (mushrooms)
150 ml (5 fl oz/⅔ cup) boiling water
3 tablespoons olive oil
3 shallots, finely chopped
2 teaspoons chopped fresh thyme
350 g (12 oz) mixed fresh mushrooms, sliced
150 ml (5 fl oz/⅔ cup) dry cider
1 bay leaf
1 teaspoon Dijon mustard
salt and pepper

Drain the barley, place in a large pan and add
the stock. Bring to the boil, cover and
simmer for 45 minutes. Soak the dried ceps
(mushrooms) in the boiling water for 20
minutes. Drain, reserving liquid, and chop
mushrooms.

Heat the oil in a large pan and fry the shallots
and thyme for 5 minutes. Add the prepared
ceps and fresh mushrooms and stir-fry over a
medium heat for 5 minutes until golden. Add
the cider and boil rapidly until liquid is
almost evaporated. Add the barley and the
coooking liquid, reserved cep (mushroom)
liquid, bay leaf and mustard to the pan and
simmer, covered, for 15 minutes. Season and
serve with fresh wholemeal rolls.

Serves 6-8.

TOMATO, OLIVE & BREAD SOUP

900 g (2 lb) very ripe tomatoes
3 tablespoons olive oil
1 onion, chopped
2 cloves garlic, crushed
115 g (4 oz) stale Italian bread, cubed
1 tablespoon chopped fresh sage
150 ml (5 fl oz/²⁄₃ cup) dry white wine
550 ml (20 fl oz/2½ cups) vegetable stock
1 tablespoon tomato purée (paste)
1 teaspoon balsamic vinegar
55 g (2 oz/½ cup) stoned black olives, finely chopped
15 g (½ oz/3 teaspoons) finely grated Parmesan cheese

Skin and seed the tomatoes over a bowl to catch any juices and finely chop the flesh; set aside. Heat the oil in a large saucepan and stir-fry the onion, garlic, bread and sage over a medium heat for 5 minutes until the bread is golden.

Add the wine and boil vigorously until almost evaporated, then stir in the tomatoes with any juices, stock, tomato purée (paste) and vinegar. Bring to the boil, cover and simmer for 15 minutes. Blend the olives and cheese together and use to garnish the soup.

Serves 6.

—CELERIAC & STILTON SOUP—

25 g (1 oz/6 teaspoons) butter
1 onion, chopped
450 g (1 lb) peeled celeriac, cubed
150 ml (5 fl oz/²⁄₃ cup) dry cider
750 ml (26 fl oz/3¼ cups) vegetable stock
1 tablespoon chopped fresh parsley
2 small red apples, cored and thickly sliced
1 tablespoon olive oil
55 g (2 oz) vegetarian Stilton cheese, crumbled
1 tablespoon chopped fresh chives
salt and pepper
parsley sprigs, to garnish

Heat the butter in a large pan and fry the onion and celeriac for 6-8 minutes until lightly golden. Add the cider and boil rapidly for 3 minutes. Add the stock and parsley, cover and cook gently for 20 minutes. Meanwhile, preheat grill.

Brush the apple slices with a little oil and grill for 1-2 minutes on each side until lightly charred. Reserve 6-8 for the garnish and add the remainder to the pan. Cook for a further 3-4 minutes, then purée the soup and cheese in a blender or food processor until smooth. Return to the pan, stir in the chives and seasoning and heat through. Transfer to warmed soup bowls, garnish with the reserved apples and parsley sprigs and serve hot.

Serves 6-8.

— CURRIED COCONUT SOUP —

2 tablespoons olive oil
1 onion, chopped
1 clove garlic, crushed
1 teaspoon grated fresh root ginger
2 teaspoons curry powder
85 g (3 oz/½ cup) long-grain rice
1.2 litres (40 fl oz/5 cups) vegetable stock
175 g (6 oz) spinach
55 g (2 oz) creamed coconut
1 tablespoon chopped fresh coriander
salt and pepper

Heat the oil in a large saucepan and fry the onion, garlic, ginger and curry powder for 5 minutes.

Add the rice and stir-fry for 2 minutes until transparent. Add the stock, bring to the boil, cover and simmer gently for 10 minutes. Wash the spinach, discard tough stalks and dry well, then cut into thin shreds. Add to the pan and cook for a further 5 minutes.

Place the creamed coconut in a small bowl and stir in 150 ml (5 fl oz/⅔ cup) boiling water, stirring until melted. Stir into the pan with the coriander and heat through for 2-3 minutes, without boiling. Taste and adjust seasoning. Serve hot.

Serves 6-8.

— AUBERGINE & GARLIC SOUP —

2 aubergines (eggplants), peeled
4 tablespoons olive oil
4 cloves garlic, peeled
55 ml (2 fl oz/¼ cup) water
1 onion, chopped
1 courgette (zucchini), chopped
2 ripe tomatoes, skinned, seeded and diced
1 teaspoon chopped fresh thyme
2 teaspoons lemon juice
850 ml (30 fl oz/3¾ cups) vegetable stock
salt and pepper
diced skinned tomatoes, grated lemon zest and thyme
   leaves, to garnish

Preheat grill. Cut the aubergines (eggplants) lengthways into 0.5 cm (¼ in) slices, brush with a little oil and place under the hot grill. Cook until lightly charred, then turn over and cook other sides also until lightly charred. Fry the garlic in 1 tablespoon oil for 5 minutes until golden, add the water, then cover and simmer for 5 minutes until soft. Mash with a fork.

Heat the remaining oil in a large saucepan and fry the onion for 3 minutes until soft. Add the courgette (zucchini), tomatoes and thyme and fry for a further 3 minutes. Add the aubergine (eggplant), mashed garlic, lemon juice and stock. Bring to the boil, cover and simmer gently for 15 minutes. Purée the soup in a blender or food processor until smooth. Return to the pan, season to taste and heat through for 5 minutes. Garnish and serve hot.

Serves 6.

— SPICED BLACK BEAN SOUP —

225 g (8 oz/1¼ cups) dried black beans, soaked
   overnight in cold water to cover
2 tablespoons olive oil
1 onion, chopped
1 clove garlic, chopped
1 dried red chilli, seeded and chopped
2 carrots, chopped
1 stick celery, chopped
1.2 litres (40 fl oz/5 cups) vegetable stock
1 teaspoon each toasted coriander seeds, cumin seeds
   and allspice
1 bay leaf
115 g (4 oz/½ cup) unsalted butter, softened
zest and juice ½ lime
1 tablespoon chopped fresh coriander
salt and pepper

Drain the soaked beans and rinse well. Heat
the oil in a large saucepan and fry the onion,
garlic, chilli, carrots and celery for 5 minutes
until browned. Add the drained beans and
stock and bring slowly to the boil. Boil for 10
minutes. Tie the spices and bay leaf in a small
piece of muslin and add to the pan. Cover
and simmer gently for 1-1¼ hours until beans
are cooked. Discard the muslin bag.

Meanwhile, prepare the lime butter. Cream
together the butter, lime zest and juice,
chopped coriander and salt and pepper to
taste. Roll into a log shape about 2.5 cm
(1 in) thick, and chill until required, then cut
into 12-16 slices. Purée the soup in a blender,
spoon into bowls and serve topped with slices
of lime butter.

Serves 6-8.

Note: For vegans, omit the lime butter.

— FRAGRANT THAI BROTH —

850 ml (30 fl oz/3 ¾ cups) vegetable stock
2 slices fresh root ginger
2 sprigs coriander
1 stalk lemon grass, lightly crushed
1 red chilli
1 clove garlic, crushed
115 g (4 oz/1 cup) diced plain tofu
2 tablespoons light soy sauce
55 g (2 oz) dried wholewheat noodles
2 carrots, peeled and cut into matchsticks
115 g (4 oz) shiitake mushrooms, wiped and sliced
2 teaspoons tamarind paste or lemon juice
coriander leaves, to garnish

Pour the stock into a pan and add the ginger, coriander sprigs, lemon grass, chilli and garlic. Bring slowly to the boil, cover and simmer gently for 25 minutes. Meanwhile, marinate the tofu in the soy sauce for 25 minutes.

Cook noodles according to packet instructions, then drain well and transfer to warmed soup bowls. Strain stock into a clean pan, add soy sauce and the tofu, carrots and mushrooms. Simmer for 2-3 minutes until tender. Arrange the tofu and vegetables over the noodles. Whisk the tamarind paste or lemon juice into the broth, return to the boil and pour over the noodles. Garnish with coriander leaves and serve at once.

Serves 4.

TOFU, LEEK & MUSHROOM SATÉ

350 g (12 oz) plain tofu
3 leeks, trimmed
12 shiitake or button mushrooms, wiped
2 tablespoons dark soy sauce
1 clove garlic, crushed
½ teaspoon grated fresh root ginger
1 small red chilli, seeded and chopped
grated zest and juice 1 lime
3 tablespoons sweet sherry
2 teaspoons clear honey
55 g (2 oz/¼ cup) crunchy peanut butter
25 g (1 oz) creamed coconut
olive oil

Cut tofu into 12 cubes and leeks into 12 thick slices and place in a shallow dish with mushrooms. Mix together the soy sauce, garlic, ginger, chilli, lime zest and juice, sherry, honey and 3 tablespoons water and pour over the tofu mixture. Marinate for several hours, stirring from time to time.

Preheat grill. Thread the tofu, leeks and mushrooms onto 8 bamboo skewers and put 150 ml (5 fl oz/⅔ cup) of the marinade into a small pan. Add the peanut butter and coconut and heat gently until melted, then stir until thickened. Brush the ingredients on the skewers with oil, pour over the remaining marinade and grill for 10-12 minutes, turning and brushing with pan juices, until golden and lightly charred. Serve with the saté sauce as a dip.

Serves 4.

— TOFU WITH TOMATO SALSA —

350 g (12 oz) smoked tofu
SALSA:
1 large, ripe beef tomato, skinned, seeded and diced
2 sun-dried tomatoes in oil, drained and chopped
1 small clove garlic, chopped
1 tablespoon chopped fresh parsley
1 tablespoon shredded fresh basil
1 small red chilli, seeded and finely chopped
1 teaspoon red wine vinegar
1/4 teaspoon sugar
4 tablespoons olive oil
salt and pepper

Drain the tofu, pat dry and cut into 12 thin slices; place in a shallow dish. Combine the fresh and dried tomatoes, garlic, herbs, chilli, vinegar and sugar in a small bowl and whisk in the oil.

Spoon tomato mixture over the sliced tofu, cover and leave to marinate for 30 minutes. Arrange on serving plates, spooning over all the juices. Sprinkle with a little salt and plenty of freshly ground black pepper.

Serves 6.

—MARINATED MOZZARELLA—

6 large cloves garlic, unpeeled
450 ml (16 fl oz/2 cups) virgin olive oil
1 teaspoon coriander seeds
1 teaspoon fennel seeds
½ teaspoon black peppercorns
400 g (14 oz) Mozzarella cheese
2 dried red chillies
2 strips lemon peel
1 sprig rosemary, bruised
1 sprig thyme, bruised
25 g (1 oz/¼ cup) black or green olives

Place the garlic cloves in a pan of cold water, bring to the boil and simmer for 15 minutes, then drain and pat dry.

Heat 1 tablespoon oil in a small frying pan and fry the garlic over a medium heat for 8-10 minutes until golden and softened. Remove with a slotted spoon and drain on kitchen paper. Dry-fry the spice seeds and peppercorns in a heavy-based frying pan for 1-2 minutes until browned; cool.

Drain and cut Mozzarella into bite-sized pieces and layer in a large jar with the garlic, fried spices, chillies, lemon peel, herbs and olives. Pour over the remaining oil, adding a little extra, to cover, if necessary, and seal the jar. Leave to marinate for several days in a cool place, but not the refrigerator, to allow time for the flavours to develop. Serve the Mozzarella and golden garlic cloves with a slice of fresh bread and a salad garnish.

Serves 6.

——————GRILLED VINE LEAVES——————

4 spring onions, finely chopped
1 small nectarine or peach, stoned and finely chopped
1 tablespoon chopped fresh mint
¼ teaspoon ground coriander
pinch of ground cumin
salt and pepper
115 g (4 oz) goat cheese
8 large vine leaves in brine, drained
olive oil for brushing

Place the onions, nectarine or peach, mint and spices in a small bowl, season and stir well until combined. Cut the cheese into 4 equal slices.

Wash and dry the vine leaves, arrange in pairs and brush the top leaves with oil. Place a slice of cheese at one end of each leaf and top with the nectarine mixture. Carefully fold the leaves over the cheese until completely covered and secure with cocktail sticks. Preheat grill.

Brush the parcels with oil, place under the hot grill and cook for 3-4 minutes on each side until leaves are lightly charred. Transfer to serving plates, carefully removing cocktail sticks and serve at once with a crisp green salad.

Serves 4.

Note: Use a low-fat cream cheese instead of the goat cheese, if preferred.

SPINACH PATTIES

450 g (1 lb) spinach leaves, washed
55 g (2 oz/¼ cup) curd cheese
15 g (½ oz/3 teaspoons) freshly grated Parmesan
  cheese
2 eggs
55 g (2 oz/1 cup) fresh white breadcrumbs
vegetable oil for frying
WALNUT SAUCE:
55 g (2 oz/⅔ cup) walnuts, toasted
4 tablespoons fresh white breadcrumbs
1 tablespoon walnut oil
85 ml (3 fl oz/⅓ cup) milk
1 teaspoon lemon juice
1 teaspoon chopped fresh tarragon
salt and pepper

In a large saucepan, cook the spinach with
only the water that clings to the leaves for
2-3 minutes until just wilted. Cool slightly,
drain and squeeze out excess liquid. Set aside
to cool completely. Meanwhile, prepare the
sauce. Place the nuts in a food processor or
blender and grind until fine. Add the breadcrumbs and oil and, with the blade running,
gradually add the milk through the funnel,
until smooth. Stir in the remaining sauce
ingredients and season to taste.

Finely chop the cooled spinach and beat in
the curd cheese and Parmesan cheese, 1 egg
and salt and pepper until mixed. Beat the
remaining egg in a small bowl. Form the
spinach mixture into 8 patties and dip first
into the egg and then into the breadcrumbs
until well coated. Heat the oil in a small
frying pan and fry the patties for 3-4 minutes
on each side until golden. Drain on absorbent
kitchen paper and serve hot, warm or cold
with the walnut sauce.

Serves 4.

—POTATO & TOMATO GALETTE—

3 potatoes, scrubbed
25 g (1 oz/6 teaspoons) butter, melted
4 ripe plum tomatoes
6 large basil leaves, shredded
salt and pepper
2 tablespoons olive oil
basil or parsley sprigs, to garnish

Preheat oven to 230C (450F/Gas 8) and lightly grease a 23 cm (9 in) pizza plate or shallow cake tin. Slice the potatoes very thinly and arrange half the quantity in circles over the base of the tin.

Brush with butter and top with the remaining potato slices. Brush again with butter, cover loosely with foil and bake for 30 minutes. Remove foil and bake for a further 15 minutes until golden.

Slice the tomatoes thinly and arrange over the potatoes. Sprinkle over the basil, season with salt and pepper and drizzle over the oil. Place under a hot grill for 3-4 minutes until bubbling. Cut into quarters and serve hot, garnished with basil or parsley.

Serves 4.

Note: For vegans, replace the butter with 2 tablespoons olive oil.

——CORN & PEPPER FRITTERS——

85 g (3 oz/²⁄₃ cup) coarse cornmeal
55 g (2 oz/¹⁄₂ cup) plain flour
salt
¹⁄₂ teaspoon sugar
1 egg, separated
115 ml (4 fl oz/¹⁄₂ cup) milk
1 tablespoon hazelnut or olive oil
150 ml (5 fl oz/²⁄₃ cup) natural yogurt
1 teaspoon lemon juice
2 teaspoons chopped fresh mint
¹⁄₄ teaspoon ground cumin
1 tablespoon chopped fresh coriander
115 g (4 oz/³⁄₄ cup) cooked sweetcorn kernels
55 g (2oz/¹⁄₂ cup) diced red pepper (capsicum)
1 teaspoon chopped green chilli
vegetable oil for frying

In a bowl, combine the cornmeal, flour and 1 teaspoon salt and the sugar. Make a well in the centre and beat in the egg yolk, milk and oil until smooth. Cover and chill for 1 hour. Blend the yogurt, lemon juice, mint, cumin and pinch of salt together; cover and chill until required. Remove the batter from the refrigerator and stir in the coriander, sweetcorn, pepper (capsicum) and chilli. Stiffly whisk the egg white and fold in until evenly incorporated.

In a small heavy-based frying pan, heat about 1 cm (¹⁄₂ in) oil until a drop of water sizzles on contact. Drop in tablespoons of the mixture in batches of 3 or 4 and fry for 1-2 minutes on each side until golden. Drain on absorbent kitchen paper and keep warm while cooking the remaining fritters in the same way. Serve hot with the minted yogurt sauce.

Makes 16.

— VEGETABLES WITH TWO OILS —

115 ml (4 fl oz/½ cup) virgin olive oil
2 cloves garlic, peeled
½ teaspoon coriander seeds, bruised
½ teaspoon fennel seeds, bruised
2 strips lemon peel
2 sprigs thyme, bruised
85 ml (3 fl oz/⅓ cup) groundnut oil
½ teaspoon sesame oil
2 slices fresh root ginger, bruised
1 small shallot, sliced
1 teaspoon soy sauce
½ teaspoon crushed dried red chillies
½ teaspoon Sechuan peppers, bruised
700 g (1½ lb) selection of baby vegetables

In a pan, heat 1 tablespoon of the olive oil and fry the whole garlic cloves, coriander and fennel seeds for 5 minutes until golden. Cool and transfer to a screw-top jar. Add the remaining olive oil, lemon peel and thyme, seal the jar and set aside. In a second jar, mix together the groundnut oil, sesame oil and all the remaining ingredients, except the vegetables for crudités. Leave both the oils to infuse for 1-2 days.

When ready to serve, transfer the two oils to small bowls. Wash and trim the vegetables as necessary and serve as crudités with the oils and slices of fresh Italian bread.

Serves 6.

Note: Choose from a selection of your favourite vegetables, such as small radishes, asparagus, broccoli, cauliflower, carrots, peppers (capsicums), celery and fennel. Lightly cooked vegetables can also be used as crudités.

——— BAKED MUSHROOMS ———

25 g (1 oz/⅓ cup) desiccated coconut
8 large open cup mushrooms, wiped
85 g (3 oz/⅓ cup) butter, softened
1 clove garlic, crushed
grated zest and juice 1 lime
½ teaspoon grated fresh root ginger
1 tablespoon chopped fresh coriander
salt and pepper

Preheat oven to 200C (400F/Gas 6). Place the coconut on a baking sheet and bake for 2-3 minutes until browned. Remove from the oven and cool slightly.

Trim the mushrooms, discard the stalks and place in a large roasting tin, trimmed-sides up. Cream the butter, coconut and remaining ingredients together and spread over the inside of the mushrooms. Cover loosely with foil and bake for 15-20 minutes until mushrooms are cooked. Serve hot with fresh bread to mop up the juices.

Serves 4.

Note: For vegans, replace the butter with 85 ml (3 fl oz/⅓ cup olive oil).

VEGETABLE FRITTERS & RELISH

2 tablespoons olive oil
½ yellow pepper (capsicum), seeded and diced
175 g (6 oz/1¼ cups) cherry tomatoes, halved
2 tablespoons red wine vinegar
1½ tablespoons sugar
3 cardamom pods, bruised
175 g (6 oz/1½ cups) plain flour
1 tablespoon chopped fresh coriander
salt
1 small aubergine (eggplant)
2 small courgettes (zucchini)
1 red pepper (capsicum), seeded
115 g (4 oz) baby sweetcorn, trimmed
12 button mushrooms
vegetable oil for deep frying
1 egg white, lightly beaten

Heat 1 tablespoon olive oil, fry the pepper (capsicum) for 2 minutes, then add the tomatoes and stir-fry for 1 minute. Add 1½ tablespoons vinegar, the sugar, cardamoms and 2 tablespoons water, boil rapidly for 5 minutes. Leave to cool. Combine the flour, coriander and 1 teaspoon salt. Beat in 225 ml (8 fl oz/1 cup) iced water and the remaining oil and vinegar to form a batter. Leave for 30 minutes. Cut the aubergine (eggplant) into thin slices, the courgettes (zucchini) into 0.5 cm (¼ in) slices and the pepper (capsicum) into thick strips.

Blanch the sweetcorn for 2 minutes, refresh under cold water and pat dry; wipe the mushrooms. Heat the vegetable oil to 180C (350F). Stiffly whisk the egg white and fold into the batter. Dip the vegetables into batter, a few at a time, shake off the excess and fry for 2 minutes until crisp and golden. Place vegetables in a warm oven and continue frying the remaining fritters. Serve hot with the sweet relish.

Serves 6.

— ARTICHOKES & MAYONNAISE —

6 large globe artichokes
1 lemon, halved
225 ml (8 fl oz/1 cup) low-calorie mayonnaise
grated zest 1 lemon
juice ½ lemon
2 tablespoons chopped fresh dill
salt and pepper
lemon zest and fresh dill sprigs, to garnish

Snap off the long stalks from artichokes and cut away the tough outer leaves. Trim and discard the top 5 cm (2 in). Drop artichokes into a large pan of boiling water, add the halved lemon, cover and cook for 30 minutes, until the leaves easily pull away. Drain artichokes and plunge into cold water. Leave until cool enough to handle.

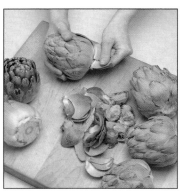

In a bowl, blend together the mayonnaise, lemon zest, juice and dill. Season to taste with salt and pepper. Scoop out the choke from each artichoke. Trim away any tough leaves that remain and cut the artichokes in half. Serve cold with the mayonnaise, garnished with grated lemon zest and dill.

Serves 6.

—FENNEL WITH FETA & PEARS—

2 fennel bulbs
4 tablespoons olive oil
175 g (6 oz) vegetarian feta cheese
1 ripe pear
4 sun-dried tomatoes in oil, drained and sliced
25 g (1 oz/¼ cup) stoned black olives
a few basil leaves
1 teaspoon lemon juice
½ teaspoon clear honey
salt and pepper

Preheat grill. Trim the fennel, discarding any damaged outer leaves. Cut each bulb, lengthways, into 6 thin slices.

Brush with a little of the olive oil and place under the hot grill for 2-3 minutes until browned. Turn fennel, brush with oil and grill for a further 2-3 minutes until charred and just tender. Leave to cool slightly.

Slice the feta into thin slabs and quarter, core and thinly slice the pear. Arrange the fennel, cheese and pear on serving plates and top with the tomatoes, olives and basil. Blend the remaining oil, lemon juice, honey and seasonings together, drizzle over the salad and serve.

Serves 4.

– CARROT & GINGER SOUFFLÉS –

45 g (1½ oz/½ cup) ground almonds, toasted
350 g (12 oz) carrots, trimmed and chopped
1 tablespoon olive oil
1 small onion, finely chopped
2 teaspoons grated fresh root ginger
45 g (1½ oz/9 teaspoons) butter
45 g (1½ oz/9 teaspoons) plain flour
225 ml (8 fl oz/1 cup) milk
55 g (2 oz) vegetarian Cheshire cheese, grated
3 eggs, separated

Preheat oven to 190C (375F/Gas 5) and lightly oil eight 225 ml (8 fl oz/1 cup) ramekin dishes.

Sprinkle the inside of each ramekin with the ground almonds to coat the sides. Shake out the excess and reserve. Cook the carrots in a pan of boiling water for 15 minutes until soft. Heat the oil in a small pan and gently fry the onion and ginger together for 10 minutes until softened. Drain the carrots and purée with the onion mixture in a blender or food processor until smooth.

Melt the butter in a small pan, stir in the flour and cook for 1 minute. Gradually add the milk, stirring, until thickened. Remove from the heat, stir in the cheese, cool and beat in the egg yolks, carrot purée and the remaining almonds. Stiffly whisk the egg whites and fold in. Spoon into the prepared ramekins, place in a roasting pan and add enough boiling water to come two-thirds of the way up the sides of the dishes. Bake for 30 minutes, then serve at once.

Serves 8.

WHITE BEAN PÂTÉ

85 g (3 oz/½ cup) dried haricot or navy beans, soaked
   overnight in cold water to cover
1 bay leaf
2 spring onions, trimmed and chopped
1 small clove garlic, chopped
2 teaspoons chopped fresh coriander
¼ teaspoon ground cumin
pinch of cayenne pepper
1 teaspoon lemon juice
1 tablespoon olive oil
salt
black olives slices, coriander sprigs and oil, to garnish

Drain the soaked beans, place in a saucepan
and cover with cold water. Add the bay leaf
and boil rapidly for 10 minutes. Lower the
heat, cover and simmer for 45-50 minutes or
until the beans are cooked. Drain, reserving 1
tablespoon of the liquid, and discard bay leaf.
Allow to cool.

Put the beans and the reserved tablespoon of
liquid into a blender or food processor. Add
all the remaining ingredients and purée to
form a smooth paste. Transfer to a bowl and
garnish with black olives and coriander and
drizzle over a little oil. Serve with toasted
pitta bread or vegetable crudités.

Serves 6-8.

- CHICKPEA & PEPPER TORTILLA -

2 tablespoons olive oil
1 red onion, chopped
1 red pepper (capsicum), seeded and chopped
2 cloves garlic, crushed
175 g (6 oz/1 cup) cooked chickpeas
1 teaspoon ground turmeric
2 tablespoons chopped fresh parsley
4 large eggs
salt and pepper
parsley sprigs, to garnish

In a non-stick frying pan, heat the oil and fry the onion, pepper (capsicum) and garlic for 10 minutes until lightly golden and softened. Add the chickpeas, mashing them lightly as you go, then stir in the turmeric and parsley. Stir-fry for 2 minutes. Lightly beat the eggs with salt and pepper and stir into the pan until evenly mixed.

Cook over a medium heat for 5-6 minutes until cooked and browned underneath. Loosen around the edges with a spatula and carefully slip the tortilla out onto a plate. Invert the pan over the tortilla and flip over so that the top is now on the bottom. Cook for a further 3-4 minutes until golden underneath and turn out onto a plate. Allow to cool to room temperature. Garnish with parsley and serve with a tomato salad.

Serves 6.

- HAZELNUT CRÊPES & SPINACH -

100 g (3½ oz/⅔ cup) plain flour
15 g (½ oz/3 teaspoons) hazelnuts, toasted and finely
   ground
salt and pepper
1 egg, lightly beaten
300 ml (10 fl oz/1¼ cups) milk
15 g (½ oz/3 teaspoons) butter, melted
175 g (6 oz) trimmed spinach, washed
175 g (6 oz/¾ cup) low-fat cream cheese
1 small clove garlic, crushed
1 tablespoon chopped fresh mixed herbs
2 tablespoons olive oil
1 teaspoon lemon juice
¼ teaspoon freshly grated nutmeg
pinch of chilli powder

Combine the flour, nuts and ½ teaspoon salt
in a bowl and gradully beat in the egg, milk
and butter to form a thin pouring batter; set
aside for 30 minutes. Heat the spinach in a
large pan, with just the water from the leaves,
for 1 minute until just wilted. Drain well,
squeeze out excess water, chop finely and
leave to cool. Beat the spinach with the low-
fat cheese, garlic, herbs, 1 tablespoon oil,
lemon juice, spices and salt and pepper to
form a paste.

Brush an omelette pan or small frying pan
with a little remaining oil and place over a
medium heat. When hot, pour in a little
batter, swirl the mixture over the base of the
pan and cook for 1-2 minutes until browned
underneath. Turn over and cook the other
side for 30 seconds, until golden. Transfer to
a plate and keep warm. Repeat to make 12
crêpes in total. Spread each one with a little
of the spinach and cheese mixture, fold up
and serve at once.

Serves 4-6.

——GRATIN OF VEGETABLES——

115 g (4 oz/²⁄₃ cup) long-grain rice
3 courgettes (zucchini)
1 red pepper (capsicum)
1 onion
6 ripe tomatoes
2 tablespoons olive oil
2 sprigs fresh thyme
2 sprigs fresh rosemary
2 bay leaves
1 teaspoon dried oregano
1 teaspoon fennel seeds, roasted
150 ml (5 fl oz/²⁄₃ cup) vegetable stock
85 g (3 oz) Pecorino or vegetarian Cheddar cheese,
    grated

Preheat oven to 200C (400F/Gas 6). Put the rice into a small pan and cover with cold water. Bring to the boil and cook for 3 minutes, drain well and transfer to a gratin dish. Thickly slice the courgettes (zucchini), roughly chop the pepper (capsicum) and onion and skin, seed and roughly chop the tomatoes.

Place the prepared vegetables in a large bowl, add the oil and stir well until vegetables are coated. Snip in the fresh herbs, add the bay leaves, oregano and fennel seeds, stir and spoon over the rice. Pour over the stock, cover with foil and bake for 40 minutes. Remove the foil, sprinkle over the cheese and return to the oven for a further 10-15 minutes until cheese is melted and all the liquid is absorbed. Brown under a hot grill, if wished, and serve hot.

Serves 6.

— MUSHROOM & BEAN CHILLI —

4 tablespoons olive oil
1 large aubergine (eggplant), diced
175 g (6 oz) button mushrooms, wiped
1 large onion, chopped
1 clove garlic, chopped
1½ teaspoons paprika
½-1 teaspoon chilli powder
1 teaspoon ground coriander
½ teaspoon ground cumin
900 g (2 lb) tomatoes, skinned and chopped
150 ml (5 fl oz/⅔ cup) vegetable stock
25 g (1 oz) tortilla chips
1 tablespoon tomato purée (paste)
400 g (14 oz) can red kidney beans
1 tablespoon chopped fresh coriander
salt and pepper

In a large pan, heat 2 tablespoons oil and stir-fry the aubergine (eggplant) for 10 minutes until golden, then remove from the pan with a slotted spoon. Add 1 tablespoon oil to the pan and stir-fry the mushrooms until golden; remove with a slotted spoon. Add the remaining oil to the pan and fry the onion, garlic and spices for 5 minutes. Add the tomatoes and stock and cook, covered, for 45 minutes.

Finely crush the tortilla chips and blend with 4 tablespoons water and the tomato purée (paste). Whisk into the chilli sauce and add the mushroom and aubergine (eggplant). Drain the beans and add to the pan with the coriander. Cover and cook for a further 20 minutes. Season to taste and serve with plain boiled rice and thick sour cream, if wished.

Serves 6.

Note: Check the packet to ensure that the tortilla chips are a vegetarian product.

PARSNIP, PEAR & ALMOND SAUTÉ

12 baby onions
3 tablespoons olive oil
575 g (1¼ lb) baby parsnips, halved or quartered
1 clove garlic, chopped
2 teaspoons chopped fresh thyme
115 ml (4 fl oz/½ cup) dry cider
150 ml (5 fl oz/⅔ cup) vegetable stock
1 tablespoon brown sugar
2 teaspoons wholegrain mustard
2 small pears, cored and thickly sliced
55 g (2 oz/½ cup) blanched almonds, toasted
salt and pepper

Place the onions in a small pan, cover with cold water and bring to the boil. Drain, refresh under cold water, peel and cut in half. Heat 2 tablespoons of the oil in a large pan and stir-fry the onions, parsnips, garlic and thyme for 10 minutes until browned all over. Add the cider and boil rapidly for 5 minutes. Blend the stock, sugar and mustard together and stir into the pan. Cover and cook for 10-12 minutes until parsnips are tender.

Meanwhile, heat the remaining oil and fry the pear slices over a high heat for 1 minute on each side until browned, then remove pears with a slotted spoon. Pour the juices from the parsnips into the pan and boil rapidly for 2-3 minutes until thickened. Pour over the parsnips, add the pears and almonds and heat through. Season to taste and serve at once.

Serves 4.

BROCCOLI CAPONATA

2 tablespoons olive oil
1 red onion, chopped
1 red pepper (capsicum), seeded and chopped
1 clove garlic, chopped
1 teaspoon chopped fresh thyme
85 ml (3 fl oz/⅓ cup) red wine
450 g (1 lb) tomatoes, skinned, seeded and chopped
150 ml (5 fl oz/⅔ cup) vegetable stock
1 tablespoon red wine vinegar
1 tablespoon brown sugar
450 g (1 lb) broccoli, trimmed and chopped
2 tablespoons tomato purée (paste)
55 g (2 oz/½ cup) stoned green olives
25 g (1 oz/¼ cup) capers, drained
1 tablespoon shredded fresh basil

In a large pan, heat the oil and fry the onion, pepper (capsicum), garlic and thyme for 6-8 minutes until lightly browned. Add the wine and boil rapidly for 3 minutes. Add the tomatoes, stock, vinegar and sugar. Stir well, then cover and simmer gently for 20 minutes.

Steam the broccoli for 5 minutes until almost cooked, add to the tomato mixture with the tomato purée (paste), olives, caper and basil. Cook for a further 3-4 minutes, remove from the heat and leave to cool. Serve at room temperature.

Serves 4.

—VEGETABLE & FRUIT CURRY—

1½ teaspoons each coriander and cumin seeds
4 tablespoons vegetable oil
1 large onion, chopped
2 carrots, chopped
2 potatoes, diced
3 cloves garlic, crushed, or 1 tablespoon garlic purée
2 teaspoons grated fresh root ginger
1 teaspoon each curry powder and turmeric
450 g (1 lb) ripe tomatoes
450 ml (16 fl oz/2 cups) vegetable stock
115 g (4 oz/1 cup) frozen peas, thawed
1 apple, cored and chopped
1 mango, peeled, stoned and chopped
85 g (3 oz/⅔ cup) cashew nuts, toasted
25 g (1 oz) creamed coconut
1 tablespoon chopped fresh coriander

In a small pan, roast the coriander and cumin seeds until browned and grind in a blender or spice grinder. Heat half the oil in a large pan and fry the onions, carrots and potatoes for 10 minutes until browned. Heat the remaining oil in a small pan and fry the garlic, ginger, ground spices, curry powder and turmeric for 5 minutes. Skin, seed and chop the tomatoes and stir into the spice mixture. Cover and cook for 10 minutes. Stir into the carrot mixture with the stock and simmer gently for 20 minutes.

Add the peas, apple and mango and cook for a further 5 minutes. Grind half the cashew nuts and mix with the creamed coconut. Stir in enough pan juices to form a paste and carefully stir into the curry until evenly combined. Heat through and serve at once, sprinkled with the whole nuts and coriander.

Serves 4-6.

TOMATO & BEAN TIAN

3 tablespoons olive oil
1 red onion, chopped
1 garlic clove, crushed
1 large red pepper (capsicum), seeded and chopped
3 teaspoons chopped fresh thyme
2 teaspoons chopped fresh rosemary
400 g (14 oz) can chopped tomatoes
432 g (15.2 oz) can cannellini beans, drained
25 g (1 oz/½ cup) each fresh breadcrumbs, chopped
  pine nuts and grated Parmesan cheese or vegetarian
  Cheddar cheese
2 large courgettes (zucchini), thinly sliced
2 ripe beef tomatoes, thinly sliced
rosemary sprigs, to garnish

Preheat oven to 190C (375F/Gas 5). In a saucepan, heat 2 tablespoons of the oil and fry the onion, garlic, pepper (capsicum), 2 teaspoons thyme and 1 teaspoon rosemary for 5 minutes. Add the tomatoes, cover and cook for 20 minutes. Stir in the beans and transfer to a shallow baking dish.

Mix the breadcrumbs, pine nuts and cheese together and sprinkle half over the tomato layer. Arrange courgettes (zucchini) and beef tomatoes in rows over the top and sprinkle over the remaining crumb mixture. Drizzle over the remaining oil and more herbs, if wished. Cover with kitchen foil and bake for 30 minutes. Remove foil and bake for a further 15-20 minutes until golden. Garnish with rosemary sprigs and serve hot with a crisp green salad.

Serves 4-6.

BUTTERNUT SQUASH CRUMBLE

700 g (1 1/2 lb) peeled butternut squash
  (about 3 small squash)
1 small fennel bulb (about 115 g/4 oz), trimmed
1 clove garlic, crushed
1 tablespoon chopped fresh sage
400 g (14 oz) can chopped tomatoes
150 ml (5 fl oz/2/3 cup) double (thick) cream
salt and pepper
115 g (4 oz/1 cup) wholemeal flour
55 g (2 oz/1/4 cup) butter, diced
55 g (2 oz/1/3 cup) macadamia nuts, chopped
25 g (1 oz/1/4 cup) grated Parmesan or vegetarian
  Cheddar cheese

Preheat oven to 200C (400F/Gas 6). Scrape
out and discard the squash seeds, cut the flesh
into 1 cm (1/2 in) pieces and place in a large
ovenproof dish. Very finely shred the fennel
and scatter over the squash with the garlic
and sage. Pour in the tomatoes and cream and
add a little salt and pepper.

Put the flour in a bowl and rub in the butter
until the mixture resembles fine breadcrumbs. Stir in the nuts and cheese and
sprinkle the crumble topping over the
squash. Cover with foil and bake in the oven
for 40 minutes. Remove foil and bake for a
further 15-20 minutes until the topping is
golden and the squash is tender.

Serves 6.

——BREAD & CHEESE PUDDING——

550 ml (20 fl oz/2½ cups) milk
1 bay leaf
2 cardamom pods, bruised
15 g (½ oz/3 teaspoons) butter
1 onion, thinly sliced
½ teaspoon chopped fresh thyme
55 g (2 oz/½ cup) drained sun-dried tomatoes,
  chopped
55 g (2 oz/¼ cup) Mascarpone cheese
225 g (8 oz) vegetarian Double Gloucester cheese,
  grated
350 g (12 oz) thinly sliced wholemeal bread
3 eggs
pinch of freshly grated nutmeg
salt and pepper

Preheat oven to 200C (400F/Gas 6) and lightly oil a 2 litre (3¾ pint/9 cup) pie dish. Put the milk, bay leaf and cardamom pods into a small pan and heat until almost boiling. Remove from the heat and leave to infuse for 10 minutes; strain into a bowl. Heat the butter and fry the onion and thyme for 10 minutes until soft. Add the tomatoes, remove from the heat, cool slightly and stir in the Mascarpone and one-quarter of the grated cheese.

Spread half the mixture over the base of the dish, top with half the bread and the remaining onion mixture. Sprinkle over half the remaining cheese, top with the rest of the bread. Whisk the eggs, nutmeg and seasonings into the milk and pour into the dish. Sprinkle over the rest of the cheese and place the dish in a roasting tin. Pour in boiling water to come two-thirds of the way up the side of the dish, cover with foil and bake for 30 minutes. Uncover and cook 20 minutes.

Serves 6-8.

– VEGETARIAN HASH POTATOES –

575 g (1¼ lb) potatoes, peeled
45 g (1½ oz/9 teaspoons) butter
1 onion, thinly sliced
1 teaspoon chopped fresh sage
1 teaspoon chopped fresh rosemary
85 ml (3 fl oz/⅓ cup) natural yogurt
45 g (1½ oz/⅓ cup) grated Cheddar cheese
1 teaspoon wholegrain mustard
1 teaspoon Worcestershire sauce

Cut potatoes into chunks, place in a pan, cover with cold water and bring to the boil. Cook for 15-20 minutes until cooked. Drain and mash roughly.

Melt 15 g (½ oz/3 teaspoons) butter in a large, non-stick frying pan and fry the onion and herbs for 10 minutes until the onion is soft and golden. Combine the remaining ingredients.

Add the mashed potatoes to the frying pan and stir in the yogurt mixture, flattening the mixture out to sides of the pan. Cook over a high heat for 5-6 minutes until golden underneath. Using a spatula, turn the hash, a little at a time, and brown the other side. Serve straight from pan.

Serves 4.

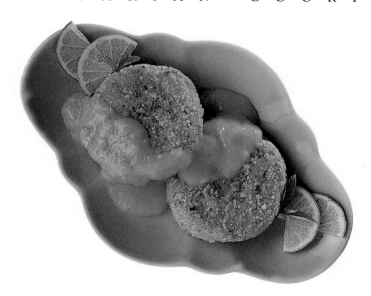

POTATO CAKES & MANGO SAUCE

225 g (8 oz) potatoes, peeled
115 g (4 oz) butternut squash, peeled
15 g (½ oz/3 teaspoons) butter, diced
1 egg yolk
45 g (1½ oz/⅓ cup) grated Cheddar cheese
1 tablespoon grated onion
2 teaspoons chopped fresh coriander
a little flour seasoned with salt and pepper
1 egg, beaten
115 g (4 oz/¾ cup) Brazil nuts, ground
115 g (4 oz) peeled mango, chopped
1 spring onion, trimmed and chopped
1 small clove garlic, crushed
½ small fresh green chilli, seeded and chopped
juice of 1 lime
vegetable oil for deep frying

Cube the potatoes and the squash and cook until tender. Drain, mash well and stir in the butter, egg yolk and cheese until melted. Stir in the onion and coriander and season to taste. Leave until cold. Shape mixture into 8 small rounds and flatten into thin patties. Dust with seasoned flour, dip in the egg and then into the ground nuts to coat the cakes on all sides.

Place all the remaining ingredients, except the oil, in a blender or food processor and purée until fairly smooth; stir in a little water if the sauce is too thick. Heat about 1 cm (½ in) vegetable oil in a non-stick frying pan and fry the potato cakes, in batches, for 2-3 minutes on each side until golden. Change the oil and repeat if necessary. Drain well on absorbent kitchen paper and serve hot with the mango sauce.

Serves 8.

—BRAISED FENNEL PROVENÇAL—

3 fennel bulbs, trimmed
3 tablespoons olive oil
4 cloves garlic, peeled
450 g (1 lb) ripe plum tomatoes, skinned, seeded and
    diced
150 ml (5 fl oz/²⁄₃ cup) dry white wine
12 Niçoise olives
4 sprigs thyme
2 bay leaves
pinch of sugar
salt and pepper
thyme sprigs, to garnish

Cut the fennel bulbs lengthways into 1 cm
(½ in) slices.

Heat the oil in a large frying pan and fry the
fennel slices and garlic for 4-5 minutes on
each side until golden; remove from pan with
a slotted spoon and reserve.

Add the tomatoes and wine to the pan and
boil rapidly for 5 minutes. Stir in the olives,
herbs and sugar and arrange the fennel slices
over the top, in a single layer, if possible.
Cover and simmer gently for 20 minutes,
season and serve hot or leave to cool and
serve at room temperature, garnished with
thyme.

Serves 4.

BAKED EGGS WITH MOZZARELLA

1 large ripe tomato
1 spring onion, trimmed and chopped
45 g (1½ oz) Mozzarella cheese, diced
4 stoned black olives, sliced
1 tablespoon chopped fresh basil
salt and pepper
85 ml (3 fl oz/⅓ cup) double (thick) cream
4 eggs
parsley sprigs, to garnish

Preheat oven to 190C (375F/Gas 5) and lightly butter 4 ramekin dishes. Skin and seed the tomato and finely dice the flesh.

Mix with the spring onion, cheese, olives, basil and seasoning. Divide between the 4 dishes.

Heat the cream in a small pan until almost boiling, pour over the tomato mixture and crack an egg into each dish. Place in a roasting tin and pour in enough boiling water to come two-thirds of the way up the sides of the ramekins. Bake for 10-15 minutes until eggs are just set. Cool slightly, garnish with parsley and serve with toasted bread fingers or Melba toast.

Serves 4.

EGG & SPINACH CUPS

225 g (8 oz) spinach
25 g (1 oz/6 teaspoons) butter, diced
25 g (1 oz) vegetarian dolcelatte cheese, crumbled
115 ml (4 fl oz/½ cup) double (thick) cream
pinch of grated nutmeg
salt and pepper
4 eggs
4 sprigs chervil (optional)

Preheat oven to 190C (375F/Gas 5) and lightly butter 4 ramekin dishes. Wash the spinach and discard any thick stalks.

Place the spinach with only the water that clings to the leaves in a large pan and cook over a medium heat for 1-2 minutes until just wilted. Drain, squeeze out excess liquid and chop finely. Transfer to a bowl and beat in the butter and cheese until melted, then stir in 85 ml (3 fl oz/⅓ cup) cream, the nutmeg and seasoning.

Divide between the ramekin dishes and make a small hollow in the centre of each one. Break an egg into each hollow and spoon over the remaining cream. Place each ramekin in a roasting pan. Pour in enough boiling water to come two-thirds of the way up the sides of the dishes and bake for 20-30 minutes until eggs feel firm to the touch. Garnish each with a chervil sprig, if wished. Serve at once with slices of crisp French bread.

Serves 4.

——— FRESH HERB FRITTATA ———

6 eggs
2 egg whites
2 spring onions, trimmed and chopped
115 g (4 oz/½ cup) cottage cheese
25 g (1 oz/½ cup) fresh chopped mixed herbs
25 g (1oz/1 cup) rocket
salt and pepper
olive oil

Whisk the eggs and the egg whites together until thoroughly mixed and stir in the spring onions, cheese and herbs. Roughly chop the rocket and add to mixture together with the seasonings.

Preheat grill. Heat about 4 teaspoons oil in a non-stick frying pan and pour in the egg mixture, swirling to reach the edges of the pan. Cook, stirring, over a medium-low heat for about 3 minutes until eggs are beginning to set.

Place pan under the hot grill and cook for a further 2-3 minutes until set and lightly golden. Turn out onto a plate, cut into wedges and serve warm or cold with a tomato and olive salad.

Serves 2-4.

CORNBREAD MUFFINS

175 g (6 oz/1 ⅓ cups) medium cornmeal
115 g (4 oz/1 cup) plain flour
25 g (1 oz/6 teaspoons) caster sugar
2 teaspoons baking powder
250 ml (9 fl oz/1 cup) buttermilk
55 g (2 oz/¼ cup) butter, melted
1 egg, lightly beaten
4 tablespoons maple syrup
fresh figs, maple syrup and crème fraîche, to serve

Preheat the oven to 200C (400F/Gas 6) and lightly oil a 12-hole muffin tin. Stir the cornmeal, flour, sugar and baking powder together in a large bowl.

Gradually beat in buttermilk, melted butter, egg and maple syrup. Beat until thick and smooth.

Spoon into the prepared muffin tin and bake for 20 minutes until muffins are risen and golden. Remove from the oven, cool slightly and turn out onto a wire rack to cool. Slice the figs into wedges and serve with the muffins, a little extra maple syrup and spoonfuls of crème fraîche.

Makes 12.

———— ITALIAN BREAD PIZZA ————

4 thick slices of Italian bread, cut from a large loaf
2 cloves garlic, halved
4 teaspoons sun-dried tomato paste
8 small plum tomatoes, thinly sliced
12-16 basil leaves, roughly shredded
150 g (5 oz) Mozzarella cheese, drained and thinly
    sliced
1 tablespoon capers in brine, drained
12 stoned green olives, halved
olive oil

Preheat oven to 240C (475F/Gas 9). Cut each slice of bread in half crossways.

Toast bread lightly on both sides. Rub all over with the garlic and spread one side of each piece with the tomato paste.

Arrange the tomatoes over the paste and sprinkle with the basil leaves. Top with the cheese, capers and olives. Drizzle a little oil over each half and bake at the top of the oven for 8-10 minutes until the cheese has melted and is golden. Serve at once with a fresh green salad.

Serves 4.

——DOLCELATTE MINI PIZZAS——

55 g (2 oz/¹/₂ cup) stoned black olives
1 clove garlic, chopped
1 teaspoon chopped fresh thyme
1 tablespoon olive oil
1 quantity pizza dough (see opposite)
45 g (1¹/₂ oz/9 teaspoons) butter
2 red onions, thinly sliced
¹/₂ teaspoon fennel seeds
1 teaspoon chopped fresh rosemary
85 g (3 oz/¹/₂ cup) vegetarian dolcelatte cheese
grated zest 1 lemon

Purée olives, garlic, thyme and oil in a blender or food processor to a smooth paste.

Make up the pizza dough (see opposite),
cover and leave to rise in a warm place for 30
minutes. Melt the butter and fry the onions
over a low heat for 20-25 minutes until
golden. Leave to cool. Preheat oven to 230C
(450F/Gas 8) and place a baking sheet or
pizza stone on the top shelf.

Divide the pizza dough in 4 and roll each
piece out on a lightly floured surface to a
12.5 cm (5 in) round. Spread over the olive
paste and onion mixture. Sprinkle over the
fennel seeds and rosemary and crumble over
the cheese. Sprinkle over the lemon zest and
transfer the pizzas to the hot baking sheet.
Cook for 10-12 minutes until bubbling and
golden. Serve the pizzas hot with a tomato
and green salad.

Serves 4.

—— GRILLED VEGETABLE PIZZA ——

225 g (8 oz/1⅔ cups) strong plain flour
½ teaspoon fast action dried yeast
½ teaspoon salt
100 ml (3½ fl oz/½ cup) warmed water
1 tablespoon olive oil
TOPPING:
1 red pepper (capsicum), quartered and seeded
1 small courgette (zucchini), sliced
1 small aubergine (eggplant), sliced
1 small onion, thinly sliced
6 large ripe tomatoes, quartered and seeded
2 tablespoons shop-bought pesto sauce
salt and pepper
150 g (5 oz) vegetarian Mozzarella cheese, grated

Mix the flour, yeast and salt together, make a well in the centre and work in the water and oil to form a stiff dough. Knead for 5 minutes, place in an oiled bowl, cover and leave to rise in a warm place for 30 minutes until doubled in size. Preheat oven to 230C (450F/Gas 8) and place a pizza plate or baking sheet on the top shelf. Preheat grill. Brush the peppers (capsicum), courgette (zucchini), aubergine (eggplant) and onion slices with a little oil and grill until charred on all sides.

Grill the tomato quarters, skin side up, until blistered. Peel and discard the skin and mash the flesh with the pesto sauce and salt and pepper. Roll out dough to a 23-25 cm (9-10 in) round. Spread over the tomato mixture and arrange the grilled vegetables over the top. Sprinkle over the cheese and transfer to the hot pizza plate or baking sheet. Bake for 25-30 minutes until bubbling and golden.

Serves 4.

- PENNE WITH LEEKS & RICOTTA -

450 g (1 lb) young leeks, washed and trimmed
2-3 tablespoons hazelnut oil
1 clove garlic, sliced
350 g (12 oz/4 cups) dried penne or other pasta shells
olive oil
225 g (8 oz/1 cup) ricotta cheese
4 tablespoons milk
45 g (1 ½ oz/⅓ cup) freshly grated Pecorino or
      Parmesan cheese
2 tablespoons mixed chopped fresh herbs
½ teaspoon grated lemon zest
½ teaspoon lemon juice
salt and pepper

Preheat oven to 220C (425F/Gas 7). Pat the
leeks dry. Cut into thick slices, place in a
roasting tin with 2 tablespoons oil and the
garlic and roast for 25 minutes until lightly
browned. After 10 minutes, bring a large pan
of water to the boil, add the pasta, a little
olive oil and return to the boil. Lower heat
and simmer gently for 10 minutes until pasta
is *al dente* (just cooked but with a firm bite).

Meanwhile, place all the remaining ingredients in a small pan and stir over a low heat
until melted. Heat through for 5 minutes
without boiling. Strain the pasta, stir in a
little more hazelnut oil and toss with the
cooked leeks. Carefully stir in the melted
cheese mixture, season to taste and serve
at once.

Serves 4.

──VEGETARIAN SPAGHETTI──

2 tablespoons hazelnut oil
55 g (2 oz/1 cup) fresh breadcrumbs
350 g (12 oz) dried spaghetti
85 ml (3 fl oz/⅓ cup) virgin olive oil
2 cloves garlic, sliced
grated zest 1 lemon
1½ teaspoons chopped fresh rosemary
450 g (1 lb) small courgettes (zucchini), thinly sliced
45 g (1½ oz/⅓ cup) drained sun-dried tomatoes in oil, sliced
2 tablespoons capers, drained
juice ½ lemon
salt and pepper

In a large non-stick frying pan, heat the hazelnut oil and stir-fry the breadcrumbs over a medium heat for 3-4 minutes until evenly browned. Remove from heat and set aside. Cook the spaghetti in a pan of boiling water, with a little added olive oil, for 8-10 minutes until *al dente* (just cooked but with a firm bite).

Heat 1 teaspoon olive oil in a large frying pan, add the garlic, lemon zest and rosemary and fry for 30 seconds until beginning to brown. Add the courgettes (zucchini) and stir-fry for 3-4 minutes until golden. Add the tomatoes and capers and cook for a further 1 minute. Stir in the lemon juice and seasonings. Drain the pasta, add the remaining olive oil and toss until well coated. Serve at once topped with the courgettes (zucchini) and breadcrumbs.

Serves 4.

CARAMELISED CABBAGE & PASTA

1 red pepper (capsicum)
55 g (2 oz/¼ cup) butter
1 large onion, thinly sliced
1 clove garlic, chopped
1 small green cabbage (about 575 g/1¼ lb)
1 tablespoon brown sugar
85 g (3 oz/1 cup) dried shell pasta
salt
chopped fresh parsley, to garnish

Preheat oven to 200C (400F/Gas 6) and roast the pepper (capsicum) whole for 20 minutes. Place in a plastic bag and leave until cool enough to handle. Peel, deseed and cut the flesh into thin strips.

In a large non-stick frying pan, melt the butter and gently fry the onion and garlic for 10 minutes until lightly browned. Trim the outer leaves off the cabbage, cut the cabbage into quarters and discard the centre core. Roughly shred the rest and stir into the pan with the sugar. Stir well, cover and cook over a very gentle heat for 15 minutes, stirring from time to time, until cabbage is golden and just tender.

Cook the pasta in lightly salted, boiling water for 10 minutes until *al dente* (just cooked but with a firm bite). Drain, and stir into the cabbage with the pepper (capsicum) and salt and pepper and serve at once, garnished with chopped parsley.

Serves 6.

Note: For vegans, replace the butter with 4 tablespoons olive oil.

- TAGLIATELLE WITH BEETROOT -

115 g (4 oz/½ cup) butter, softened
2 tablespoons chopped fresh chives
1 teaspoon grated lemon zest
2 tablespoons walnut oil
1 large onion, thinly sliced
1 teaspoon sugar
2 teaspoons balsamic vinegar
450 g (1 lb) cooked beetroot, diced
525 g (1 lb 2 oz) fresh tagliatelle
salt and pepper
small bunch fresh chervil, chopped

Cream the butter, chives and lemon zest together, and chill for 1 hour.

In a non-stick frying pan, heat the oil and fry the onion over a medium heat for 15 minutes until evenly golden. Add the sugar, vinegar and beetroot and stir in three-quarters of the chive butter. Cover and cook gently for 4-5 minutes.

Cook the pasta in boiling water for 3-4 minutes until *al dente* (just cooked but with a firm bite). Drain well, season with salt and plenty of freshly ground black pepper and stir in the remaining chive butter to thoroughly coat the pasta. Toss with the beetroot and onion mixture and serve at once, sprinkled with the chervil.

Serves 4.

──── RADICCHIO RISOTTO ────

2 tablespoons olive oil
1 large onion, chopped
1 large clove garlic, chopped
1 teaspoon chopped fresh thyme
350 g (12 oz/2 cups) risotto rice
1 large head radicchio, shredded
150 ml (5 fl oz/⅔ cup) red wine
550 ml (20 fl oz/2½ cups) vegetable stock
2 tablespoons sun-dried tomato paste
salt and pepper
chopped fresh parsley, to garnish
freshly grated Parmesan cheese, to serve

In a large, heavy-based, non-stick frying pan, heat the oil and fry the onion, garlic and thyme for 5 minutes until softened. Add the rice and stir over a medium heat for 1 minute, until rice is transparent. Stir in the radicchio and immediately add the wine. Boil rapidly until all the liquid has evaporated.

Gradually add the stock in 3-4 batches, simmering over a low heat for 25 minutes or until all the stock is absorbed and the rice is tender. Stir in the tomato paste and seasoning. Garnish with chopped parsley. Serve hot with plenty of grated Parmesan cheese.

Serves 6-8.

Note: For a vegan recipe, omit the cheese.

——LEEK & MUSHROOM PILAF——

15 g (½ oz/¼ cup) dried ceps (mushrooms)
pinch of saffron strands
150 ml (5 fl oz/⅔ cup) boiling water
225 g (8 oz/1¼ cups) basmati rice
450 ml (16 fl oz/2 cups) vegetable stock
2 tablespoons olive oil
3 large leeks, trimmed
115 g (4 oz) fresh mushrooms, wiped
salt and pepper
whole or chopped chives, to garnish

Place the ceps and saffron in a small bowl and pour over the boiling water. Leave to soak for 10 minutes.

Wash the rice under cold running water for several minutes until the water runs clear and drain well. Place in a saucepan and add the stock and cep mixture. Bring to the boil, stir once, cover and simmer gently for 12 minutes.

Meanwhile, heat the oil and fry the leeks for 3 minutes, then add the fresh mushrooms and stir-fry for a further 3 minutes; keep warm. As soon as the rice is cooked, stir it into the pan and heat through for 1-2 minutes. Season, garnish with chives and serve at once.

Serves 6.

——LEMON VEGETABLE RICE——

juice 2 lemons
2 tablespoons caster sugar
vegetable stock (see method)
300 g (10 oz/1 ½ cups) long-grain rice
½ teaspoon salt
1 cinnamon stick
5 whole cloves
25 g (1 oz/6 teaspoons) butter
1 teaspoon cumin seeds
1 small onion, thinly sliced
2 small courgettes (zucchini)
55 g (2 oz/⅓ cup) cashew nuts, toasted
2 tablespoons chopped fresh mint

Mix the lemon juice and sugar together in a measuring jug. Make up to 550 ml (20 fl oz/ 2½ cups) with vegetable stock. Pour into a saucepan, add the rice, salt, cinnamon and cloves, bring to the boil, stir once and cook gently for 10 minutes until all the liquid is absorbed. Remove from the heat, cover with a tight-fitting lid and leave to sit undisturbed for a further 10 minutes.

In a small frying pan, melt the butter and stir-fry the cumin seeds for 1-3 minutes until they start to pop. Add the onion and fry for 5 minutes. Cut the courgettes (zucchini) into thin slices and add to the pan with the cashew nuts and mint. Stir-fry for 2-3 minutes until courgettes (zucchini) are tender, then stir in the rice. Heat through for 1 minute and serve.

Serves 4-6.

Note: For vegans, replace the butter with 2 tablespoons olive oil.

— MUSHROOM & CHEESE PIES —

1 kg (2 lb) made puff pastry
7 g (¼ oz) dried ceps (mushrooms)
150 ml (5 fl oz/⅔ cup) boiling water
2 tablespoons olive oil
115 g (4 oz) aubergine (eggplant), diced
225 g (8 oz) mixed mushrooms, wiped and finely
   chopped
1 clove garlic, crushed
1 teaspoon chopped fresh thyme
2 tablespoons tomato purée (paste)
salt and pepper
45 g (1½ oz) vegetarian goat cheese, diced
1 egg, beaten
1 tablespoon milk

Roll out the pastry into two 23 x 32.5 cm (9 x 13 in) rectangles and cut six 10 cm (4 in) squares from each one. Cover and leave to rest for 30 minutes. Place ceps in a bowl, pour over the boiling water and leave to soak for 20 minutes. Drain, reserve stock and chop and reserve ceps. Heat 1 tablespoon oil in a large pan, stir-fry the aubergine (eggplant) for 3-4 minutes, add the ceps, fresh mushrooms, garlic and thyme and stir-fry for a further 3 minutes. Add the reserved cep liquid and boil rapidly for 3 minutes. Stir in the tomato purée (paste) and seasonings; cool.

Preheat oven to 220C (425F/Gas 7). Spread a large spoonful of the mushroom mixture in the centre of 6 pastry squares, leaving a narrow border around the edges. Top with the diced cheese. Dampen the edges with a little water and top with the remaining pastry. Press edges together to seal and cut a small slit in the top of each pie. Beat the egg and milk together and brush over each pie. Transfer to a baking sheet and cook for 15-18 minutes until puffed and golden.

Serves 6.

—— VEGETABLE FILO PARCELS ——

4 small new potatoes, halved
8 baby carrots, trimmed
8 baby courgettes (zucchini), halved
8 asparagus tips, trimmed
1 baby leek, trimmed and sliced into 8
55 g (2 oz/¼ cup) butter, softened
1 tablespoon chopped fresh mint
¼ teaspoon ground cumin
pinch of cayenne pepper
salt and pepper
4 large sheets filo pastry
85 ml (3 fl oz/⅓ cup) olive oil

Preheat oven to 190C (375F/Gas 5) and place a baking sheet on the middle shelf.

Cook the potatoes in boiling water for 6-8 minutes until almost cooked. Blanch the remaining vegetables for 2-3 minutes, depending on the size, until almost tender. Drain all the vegetables, plunge into cold water, allow to cool, then drain and dry thoroughly. Cream together the butter, mint, spices and salt and pepper. Take one large sheet of pastry and using a 25 cm (10 in) plate or saucepan lid as a template, carefully cut out a circle; repeat to make 4 in total. Brush liberally with oil.

Take a quarter of the vegetables and place a small pile on one side of the pastry circle. Dot with the mint butter and fold the other side of pastry over the filling, pressing the edges together well. Brush a little oil along the edge and turn over a bit at a time to ensure filling is totally enclosed. Repeat to make 4 parcels and transfer to the heated baking sheet. Carefully brush over remaining oil and bake for 12-15 minutes until pastry is golden. Serve immediately

Serves 4.

──GOAT CHEESE & FIG TART──

200 g (7 oz/1¾ cups) plain flour
pinch of salt
115 g (4 oz/½ cup) butter
1 egg yolk
2 tablespoons iced water
1 tablespoon olive oil
1 large onion, thinly sliced
2 teaspoons chopped fresh thyme
½ teaspoon fennel seeds
4 fresh figs
115 g (4 oz/½ cup) soft goat cheese
25 g (1 oz/¼ cup) freshly grated Parmesan cheese
150 ml (5 fl oz/⅔ cup) thick sour cream
1 large egg, lightly beaten

Preheat oven to 200C (400F/Gas 6). Sift the flour and salt into a bowl and rub in the butter until mixture resembles fine breadcrumbs. Make a well in the centre and work in the egg yolk and water to form a soft dough. Knead on a floured surface, wrap and chill for 30 minutes. Roll out thinly and use to line a 23 cm (9 in) tart tin. Prick the base and chill for 20 minutes. Line with foil and baking beans and bake blind for 10 minutes; remove foil and beans and bake for a further 10-12 minutes until crisp and golden.

Heat the oil and fry the onions, thyme and fennel for 10 minutes. Chop 2 figs, add to the pan and remove from the heat. Beat the goat cheese, Parmesan, cream and egg together until smooth. Spread the onion mixture into tart case and spoon in the cheese mixture. Slice the remaining figs and arrange around the outside of the tart. Bake for 25 minutes until risen and set. Leave to cool and serve warm or cold.

Serves 8.

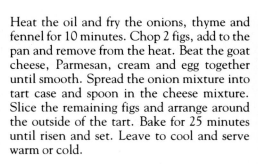

POTATO & ONION FLAN

200 g (7 oz/1¾ cup) plain flour
pinch of salt
100 g (3½ oz) unsalted butter, diced
1 egg yolk
2 tablespoons iced water
FILLING:
450 g (1 lb) waxy potatoes
25 g (1 oz/6 teaspoons) butter
2 large onions, thinly sliced
1 teaspoon chopped fresh rosemary
½ teaspoon caraway seeds
200 ml (7 fl oz/1 cup) low-fat fromage frais
25 g (1 oz/¼ cup) grated vegetarian Cheddar cheese
freshly grated nutmeg

Preheat oven to 200C (400F/Gas 6). Sift the flour and salt into a large bowl and rub in the butter until mixture resembles fine bread-crumbs. Make a well in the centre, work in the egg yolk and water to form a soft dough. Knead on a floured surface, wrap and chill for 30 minutes. Roll out thinly and use to line a deep 23 cm (9 in) fluted flan tin. Prick the base, then chill for 20 minutes. Line with foil and baking beans and bake blind for 10 minutes; remove beans and foil and bake for a further 10-12 minutes until crisp.

Increase oven temperature to 230C (450F/ Gas 8). Cook the potatoes for 15 minutes until just tender. Allow to cool, carefully peel and cut into very thin slices. Melt the butter and fry the onions, rosemary and caraway seeds for 10 minutes until golden. Spread the onion mixture over pastry case and arrange the potato slices over the top. Beat the remaining ingredients together, spread over the potatoes and bake at the top of the oven for 15 minutes until golden.

Serves 6-8.

—OLIVE & MOZZARELLA PUFFS—

55 g (2 oz/½ cup) stoned green olives
25 g (1 oz) Mozzarella cheese
2 teaspoons chopped fresh parsley
½ teaspoon chopped fresh sage
pinch of chilli powder
225 g (8 oz) bought puff pastry, thawed if frozen
1 egg
salt

Preheat oven to 220C (425F/Gas 7) and lightly oil a baking sheet. Very finely chop the olives and cheese and mix with the herbs and chilli powder to form a paste. Set aside.

Roll out the pastry thinly and stamp out 8 rounds, using a 10 cm (4 in) fluted pastry cutter. Place a heaped teaspoon of olive mixture in the centre of each round. Lightly dampen the edges of pastry, fold in half to form semi-circles, pressing edges together well to seal. Transfer to the baking sheet.

Beat the egg with a little salt and brush over pastries. Cut 2 small slashes in each one and bake for 12-15 minutes until puffed up and golden. Serve warm or cold with a salad garnish.

Serves 8.

Note: These make ideal buffet party nibbles. Make up double quantity of the filling, cut pastry into small rounds to make bite-sized appetizers.

—— WINTER VEGETABLE PIE ——

175 g (6 oz/1¼ cups) self-raising flour
salt
115 g (4 oz/½ cup) hard white vegetable fat, divided
    into 4
2 tablespoons chopped fresh mixed herbs
4-5 tablespoons iced water
175 g (6 oz) baby onions, halved
1 clove garlic, chopped
575 g (1¼ lb) prepared mixed winter vegetables
    (carrots, turnips, parsnips, cauliflower flowerets)
115 g (4 oz) button mushrooms, wiped
2 tablespoons olive oil
150 ml (5 fl oz/⅔ cup) red wine
350 ml (12 fl oz/1½ cups) vegetable stock (see Note)
2 tablespoons tomato purée (paste)

Sift the flour with 1 teaspoon salt and finely
rub in one-quarter of the fat. Stir in half the
herbs and work in enough iced water to form
a soft dough. Knead lightly, wrap and chill for
30 minutes. Roll out pastry to a rectangle
about 1 cm (½ in) thick, dot the top two-
thirds with one-third of the remaining fat.
Bring the bottom third of pastry up into the
middle and the top third down over this.
Press edges to seal, cover and chill for 30
minutes. Repeat the process twice and chill
for a final 30 minutes.

Preheat oven to 200C (400F/Gas 6). Fry
onions, garlic and the vegetables in the oil for
10 minutes. Add the wine and boil for 5
minutes. Add the stock and tomato purée
(paste) and simmer for 20 minutes. Transfer
to a 1.2 litre (2 pint/5 cup) pie dish.

Roll pastry out to a 0.5 cm (¼ in) rectangle, cut out a pie top a little larger than the dish. Cut remaining pastry into strips, dampen and press around edge of dish. Dampen edge of pastry, place pastry lid over pie and press edges to seal. Bake in the oven for 30 minutes.

Serves 6.

Note: To make your own stock, fry 1 roughly chopped onion and 1 trimmed and sliced leek in 2 teaspoons olive oil until softened. Add 2 chopped carrots, 1 diced large potato and 2 sliced sticks celery and fry for a further 5 minutes.

Add 4 roughly chopped ripe tomatoes, 115 g (4 oz) quartered mushrooms, 55 g (2 oz/ ⅓ cup) rice, 2 sprigs parsley, 2 sprigs thyme, 1 bay leaf, 1 teaspoon salt, 6 white peppercorns and 1.2 litres (2 pints/5 cups) water. Bring to the boil, cover and simmer gently for 30 minutes. Strain through a fine sieve.

—— BROCCOLI & OLIVE FLAN ——

225 g (8 oz) home-made or bought wholemeal pastry,
   thawed if frozen
1 yellow pepper (capsicum)
1 red pepper (capsicum)
115 g (4 oz) broccoli flowerets
55 g (2 oz/½ cup) stoned black olives, halved
2 eggs, beaten
115 ml (4 fl oz/½ cup) single (light) cream
115 g (4 oz/½ cup) soft goat cheese
2 tablespoons chopped fresh parsley
salt and pepper

Roll out the pastry on a lightly floured surface
and use to line a deep 23 cm (9 in) fluted flan
tin. Prick the base and chill for 20 minutes.
Preheat the oven to 200C (400F/Gas 6).
Quarter and seed the peppers (capsicums)
and grill for 4-5 minutes on each side until
lightly charred. Leave to cool slightly, then
peel and thinly slice the flesh. Steam the
broccoli for 3 minutes.

Line the flan case with foil and baking beans
and bake blind for 10 minutes; remove beans
and foil and bake for a further 10-12 minutes
until pastry is crisp and golden. Cool slightly
and arrange peppers (capsicums), broccoli
and olives over the base. Beat the remaining
ingredients together until smooth and pour
into the case. Bake for 35 minutes until risen
and firm in the centre. Cool and serve warm
or cold.

Serves 6-8.

—— SPINACH RISOTTO CAKE ——

a pinch of saffron strands
700 ml (25 fl oz/3 ¼ cups) hot vegetable stock
55 g (2 oz/¼ cup) butter
1 large onion, finely chopped
1 clove garlic, crushed
225 g (8 oz/1 ⅓ cups) risotto rice
225 g (8 oz) spinach, washed and trimmed
2 eggs, lightly beaten
55 g (2 oz/¼ cup) mascarpone cheese or thick sour
   cream
25 g (1 oz/¼ cup) grated vegetarian Cheddar cheese
1 tablespoon chopped fresh tarragon
pinch of grated nutmeg
salt and pepper

Soak the saffron strands in the hot stock for 10 minutes. Melt the butter in a large frying pan and fry the onion and garlic for 10 minutes. Add rice and stir-fry for 2 minutes. Add a little stock, simmer until absorbed and continue adding stock gradually until completely absorbed and rice is tender – about 25 minutes. Preheat oven to 200C (400F/Gas 6) and lightly oil a 20 cm (8 in) spring-release tin.

Cook the spinach in a large pan with only the water that clings to the leaves until just wilted. Drain well and squeeze out excess liquid; chop finely. Beat all the remaining ingredients together until combined and stir into the cooked rice with the spinach. Transfer to the prepared tin, smooth the surface and bake for 30 minutes until risen.

Serves 8.

Note: Serve with a double quantity of Red Pepper (Capsicum) Sauce (see page 73).

— WHOLE SWEETCORN BREAD —

225 g (8 oz/1²⁄₃ cups) coarse cornmeal
225 g (8 oz/2 cups) plain flour
1 teaspoon fast action dried yeast
1 teaspoon sugar
½ teaspoon salt
200 g (7 oz) can sweetcorn kernels
150 ml (5 fl oz/²⁄₃ cup) milk
25 g (1 oz/6 teaspoons) butter, melted

Combine the cornmeal, flour, yeast, sugar and salt in a large bowl and make a well in the centre.

Drain the sweetcorn, reserve the juices and pour into a small pan. Add the milk and heat gently until tepid. Stir into the cornmeal mixture with the melted butter and gradually work to form a soft dough. Knead on a lightly floured surface for 6-8 minutes until smooth, then carefully begin working in the sweetcorn kernels, adding a little more flour, if necessary. Place in an oiled bowl, cover and leave to rise in a warm place for 45 minutes until doubled in size.

Preheat oven to 220C (425F/Gas 7). Knock back risen dough, form into a log shape and press into an oiled 23 x 12.5 cm (9 x 5 in) loaf tin. Cover and leave to rise for 30 minutes until dough reaches the top of the tin. Bake for 25 minutes until risen and golden and the base sounds hollow when tapped. Leave to cool on a wire rack before serving.

Makes 1 large loaf.

Note: For vegans, replace butter with 2 tablespoons oil and use soya milk.

— POLENTA WITH MUSHROOMS —

850 ml (30 fl oz/3¾ cups) vegetable stock
½ teaspoon salt
150 g (5 oz/1 cup) polenta
1 teaspoon chopped fresh thyme
25 g (1 oz/¼ cup) freshly grated Parmesan or Cheddar
 cheese
25 g (1 oz/6 teaspoons) butter
15 g (½ oz/¼ cup) dried ceps (mushrooms)
85 ml (3 fl oz/⅓ cup) boiling water
55 ml (2 fl oz/¼ cup) port
3 tablespoons virgin olive oil
1 clove garlic, crushed
1 shallot, finely chopped
350 g (12 oz) mixed fresh mushrooms, sliced
1 tablespoon chopped fresh parsley

Bring 700 ml (25 fl oz/3¼ cups) of the stock and the salt to the boil in a pan and immediately whisk in the polenta. Stir, cover and simmer gently for 25 minutes, stirring frequently. Add the thyme and cook for a further 5 minutes. Stir in the cheese and butter and pour into a lightly oiled, shallow tin. Smooth the surface and leave to cool. Soak the ceps in the boiling water for 20 minutes. Strain liquid into a pan and chop the ceps. Add the port and the remaining stock to the pan and boil until reduced to about 115 ml (4 fl oz/½ cup). Set aside.

Turn out polenta and cut into 12 triangles, brush with oil and grill for 8-10 minutes on each side until golden. Meanwhile, heat the oil in a large pan and fry the garlic, shallot and ceps for 5 minutes. Add the fresh sliced mushrooms and stir-fry for 3-4 minutes until golden. Add the reduced liquid, cover and cook for 5 minutes. Add parsley and serve sauce with the grilled polenta triangles.

Serves 6.

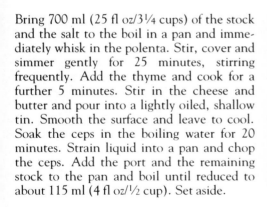

— PASTA & SQUASH TRIANGLES —

175 g (6 oz/1½ cups) plain flour
1 teaspoon salt
6 sage leaves, chopped
2 eggs
1 egg yolk
3 tablespoons olive oil
shavings of Parmesan cheese, to serve
FILLING:
225 g (8 oz) peeled butternut squash, cubed
1 small clove garlic, crushed
85 g (3 oz/⅓ cup) ricotta cheese
55 g (2 oz/½ cup) freshly grated Parmesan cheese
pinch of grated nutmeg
salt and pepper

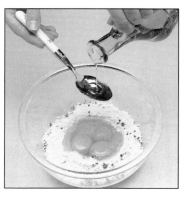

In a large bowl, mix the flour, salt and sage. Make a well in the centre and work in the eggs, egg yolk and 1 tablespoon oil to form a stiff dough. Knead on a lightly floured surface for 5 minutes until smooth and elastic. Wrap in cling film and leave to rest for 30 minutes.

Prepare the filling. Steam the squash for 10-15 minutes until soft. Mash with a fork until smooth, transfer to a clean pan and heat gently until completely dry. Place in a bowl and leave until cold. Beat in the garlic, ricotta and Parmesan cheeses, nutmeg and seasoning to taste.

Divide the pasta dough into 4 pieces and roll out each piece on a lightly floured surface as thinly and evenly as possible. Cut into 7.5 cm (3 in) squares.

Place a teaspoon of the squash filling in the middle of each square, dampen the edges and fold in half, diagonally, to form triangles. Transfer the triangles to a floured tray, or tea-towel, to prevent them sticking together.

Bring a large pan of salted water to a rolling boil, add 1 tablespoon of the remaining olive oil and cook the triangles in batches for 3-5 minutes until cooked. Drain and toss with extra olive oil and serve with shavings of Parmesan and black pepper.

Serves 4-6.

Note: The pasta dough can be made in a food processor using a dough blade. If you have a pasta machine, roll the dough out to the thinnest setting.

NOODLES WITH ROASTED TOFU

350 g (12 oz) plain tofu, cubed
2 tablespoons dark soy sauce
1 clove garlic, crushed
1 teaspoon grated fresh root ginger
1 teaspoon sesame oil
1 teaspoon clear honey
450 ml (16 fl oz/2 cups) vegetable stock
1 stalk lemon grass, crushed
2 star anise
1 red chilli
1 tablespoon olive oil
55 g (2 oz) each asparagus tips, oyster mushrooms,
    mange tout (snow peas), Chinese cabbage, trimmed
225 g (8 oz) fresh pasta noodles
1 tablespoon miso paste

Place cubed tofu in a baking dish. Mix together the soy sauce, garlic, ginger, sesame oil and honey and pour over tofu. Leave to marinate for 2-4 hours, stirring from time to time. Preheat oven to 200C (400F/Gas 6). Strain tofu, reserve 1 tablespoon marinade and transfer the tofu to the oven. Roast for 30 minutes, turning once, until crisp and golden. Put stock, reserved marinade, lemon grass, star anise and chilli in a pan, bring to the boil, cover and simmer gently for 25 minutes.

Heat the oil in a wok or large frying pan and stir-fry the asparagus for 2 minutes, add remaining vegetables and stir-fry for a further 1 minute. Cook the pasta noodles according to packet instructions. Strain the stock into the wok and stir in the miso paste until combined. Strain pasta, add to the pan and stir in the roasted tofu and pan juices. Serve at once.

Serves 4.

Note: For vegans, replace honey with sugar.

WATERCRESS CUSTARDS

2 red peppers (capsicums)
2 tablespoons olive oil
115 ml (4 fl oz/½ cup) vegetable stock
15 g (½ oz/3 teaspoons) butter
115 g (4 oz) watercress leaves
3 eggs
200 ml (7 fl oz/¾ cup) double (thick) cream
25 g (1 oz/¼ cup) finely grated vegetarian Cheddar
    cheese
1 teaspoon Dijon mustard
salt and pepper

Preheat oven to 200C (400F/Gas 6) and roast
the peppers (capsicums) for 20-25 minutes
until skins are lightly charred. Transfer to a
plastic bag and leave to cool for 30 minutes.
Peel the peppers, discard the seeds, reserving
any juices. Purée the peppers (capsicums)
and juices with the oil and stock to form a
smooth sauce. Pass through a sieve into a
small pan. Reduce oven temperature to 180C
(350F/Gas 4) and grease 6 dariole moulds.

Melt the butter and fry the watercress leaves
for 1 minute until just wilted. Purée in a
blender or food processor and gradually add
the eggs, cream, cheese, mustard and salt and
pepper until smooth. Pour into the moulds.
Place in a roasting tin and pour in enough
boiling water to come two-thirds the way up
the sides of the moulds. Bake for 25 minutes
until firm in the centre. Leave to rest for 5
minutes, then unmould and serve warm with
the reheated pepper sauce.

Serves 6.

SPINACH GNOCCHI

350 g (12 oz) trimmed spinach leaves
175 g (6 oz/¾ cup) ricotta cheese
pinch of freshly grated nutmeg
45 g (1½ oz/⅓ cup) plain flour
1 large egg, lightly beaten
25 g (1 oz/¼ cup) grated Parmesan or vegetarian
    Cheddar cheese
2 tablespoons olive oil
salt and pepper
400 g (14 oz) can chopped tomatoes
1 clove garlic, crushed
1 tablespoon chopped fresh basil
pinch of sugar
115 g (4 oz) vegetarian dolcelatte cheese
2 tablespoons milk

Wash the spinach and wilt in a large pan over medium heat. Drain, squeeze out excess liquid and chop finely. Cool and beat in the ricotta, nutmeg, flour, egg, cheese, half the oil and salt and pepper. Chill for 2 hours.

Put tomatoes, remaining oil, garlic, basil and sugar in a small saucepan and cook gently for 30 minutes. Purée in a blender or food processor and keep warm.

Shape the ricotta mixture into walnut-sized balls, flatten out and place on a floured tray, to make 32 small gnocchi in total.

Bring a large pan of water to a steady simmer, drop in the gnocchi, in batches, and cook for 6 minutes. Drain on absorbent kitchen paper and keep warm while cooking the remainder in the same way. Preheat grill.

Gently heat the milk and dolcelatte, stirring until smooth. Pour the tomato sauce over the base of 4 gratin dishes or flameproof plates, arrange the gnocchi on top and drizzle over the cheese sauce. Place dishes under a hot grill for 3-4 minutes until bubbling and golden.

Serves 4.

- CHICORY-ASPARAGUS GRATIN -

20 asparagus spears
4 small heads chicory
115 ml (4 fl oz/½ cup) virgin olive oil
1 clove garlic, crushed
grated zest and juice ½ lemon
1 tablespoon chopped fresh basil
45 g (1½ oz/⅓ cup) freshly grated Parmesan or
    Cheddar cheese
salt and pepper

Trim the asparagus spears, removing the woody ends, and peel almost to the tips. Steam the spears for 2 minutes until bright green.

Lightly oil 4 small gratin dishes. Preheat grill. Halve and trim the chicory and place 2 halves into each dish. Arrange the asparagus between the chicory.

Mix together the oil, garlic, lemon zest and juice and basil and pour over the vegetables. Place under a hot grill and cook for 3-4 minutes. Sprinkle over the cheese and return to the grill for 2-3 minutes until golden. Season and serve at once.

Serves 4.

——OLIVE & TOMATO SALAD——

700 g (1½ lb) mixed yellow and green courgettes
  (zucchini)
1 tablespoon olive oil
115 g (4 oz/¾ cup) cherry tomatoes, halved
55 g (2 oz/⅓ cup) stoned black olives, chopped
1 small oak leaf lettuce
15 g (½ oz/3 teaspoons) pine nuts, toasted
DRESSING:
3 tablespoons olive oil
1 teaspoon balsamic vinegar
½ clove garlic, crushed
½ teaspoon chopped fresh thyme
salt and pepper

Preheat oven to 220C (425F/Gas 7). Wash
and trim the courgettes (zucchini) and cut
into 2.5 cm (1 in) thick slices. Place in a
roasting tin, toss with the oil and bake at the
top of the oven for 20 minutes until tender.

Place the tomatoes and olives in a large bowl
and stir in the cooked courgettes (zucchini).
Blend the dressing ingredients together, add
to the bowl and stir well. Leave until the
courgettes (zucchini) are cold. Wash and
trim the lettuce, discarding the tough outer
leaves, and tear into bite-sized pieces.
Arrange the lettuce on 4 serving plates.
Spoon over the salad with all the juices and
sprinkle over the pine nuts. Serve at once.

Serves 4.

——LETTUCE & EGG SALAD——

12 quail eggs or 3 hen eggs
6 Little Gem lettuces
85 g (3 oz/3 cups) watercress
3 spring onions, trimmed
25 g (1 oz) Parmesan or vegetarian Cheddar cheese
25 g (1 oz) chervil, roughly shredded
DRESSING:
3 tablespoons virgin olive oil
2 teaspoons Champagne vinegar
salt and pepper

Cook the quail eggs for 3 minutes or the hen eggs for 12 minutes, then plunge immediately into cold water. Peel and then cut into halves or quarters.

Trim and discard the outer leaves of the lettuces and cut each lettuce into quarters. Discard any thick stalks from the watercress, then wash and pat dry. Thinly slice the spring onions. Divide the lettuce quarters, watercress and onions between 4 serving plates and, using a potato peeler, shave a little Parmesan or Cheddar over each. Sprinkle with the chervil and garnish each salad with the cooked eggs.

Blend the dressing ingredients together until combined, pour the dressing over the salads and serve at once.

Serves 4.

—VEGETARIAN CAESAR SALAD—

2 tablespoons mayonnaise
1 tablespoon vodka
1 tablespoon lime juice
1 teaspoon Worcestershire sauce or 2 drops Tabasco
150 ml (5 fl oz/⅔ cup) light olive oil
1 tablespoon chopped fresh mint
1 tablespoon chopped fresh parsley
½ teaspoon ground cumin
¼ teaspoon chilli powder
1 small clove garlic, crushed
two 1 cm (½ in) slices day-old bread
2 Cos lettuces
115 g (4 oz/¾ cup) grated Cheshire cheese

Preheat the oven to 190C (375F/Gas 5). Blend the mayonnaise, vodka, lime juice, Worcestershire sauce or Tabasco together and whisk in 85 ml (3 fl oz/⅓ cup) oil, a little at a time, until thickened slightly. Stir in half the herbs and set aside. Mix remaining oil and herbs, the spices and garlic together and brush over both sides of the bread. Place on a wire rack or trivet and bake for 10-12 minutes. Turn bread and continue cooking for a further 10-12 minutes until crisp and golden on both sides. Cool slightly and cut into cubes.

Just before serving, wash the lettuce, discarding the outer leaves, and dry well. Place in a large bowl, stir in the croûtons and cheese, add the dressing and toss well until evenly coated.

Serves 4.

—SESAME-DRESSED CHICORY—

DRESSING:
70 ml (2½ fl oz/⅓ cup) light olive oil
½ teaspoon sesame oil
2 teaspoons orange juice
1 teaspoon balsamic vinegar
1 teaspoon grated fresh root ginger
½ teaspoon grated orange zest
½ teaspoon clear honey
salt and pepper
SALAD:
6 heads of chicory, trimmed and halved
115 g (4 oz) French beans, trimmed
3 teaspoons sesame seeds, toasted

To prepare the dressing, place all the ingredients in a screw top jar and shake vigorously. Leave in a cool place for the flavours to develop. Preheat grill.

Wash and dry the chicory, brush with a little dressing and place under the hot grill to cook for 3-4 minutes on each side until leaves become lightly charred. Meanwhile, blanch the beans in boiling water for 1-2 minutes until just tender. Drain, refresh under cold water and pat dry. Arrange 3 chicory halves on each plate, add the beans, drizzle over the dressing and sprinkle with the sesame seeds. Serve at once.

Serves 4.

—ORIENTAL CARROT SALAD—

350 g (12 oz) carrots, scrubbed
3 tablespoons peanut oil
½ teaspoon sesame oil
1 teaspoon grated fresh root ginger
1 small clove garlic, sliced
1 dried red chilli, seeded and crushed
2 tablespoons lemon juice
1 teaspoon sugar
55 g (2 oz/⅓ cup) raw peanuts, toasted and chopped
salt and pepper
coriander leaves, to garnish

Finely grate the carrots and place in a large bowl.

Heat 1 tablespoon peanut oil with the sesame oil and fry the ginger, garlic and chilli until just turning golden. Whisk in the remaining oil, lemon juice and sugar and remove from the heat.

Pour the dressing over the carrots, add the nuts and toss well until evenly combined. Cover and leave to marinate for 30 minutes. Stir again, season to taste and serve garnished with coriander leaves.

Serves 4.

—WILD & BROWN RICE SALAD—

115 g (4 oz/1 cup) wild rice
salt
175 g (6 oz/1¼ cups) brown rice
55 g (2 oz/⅔ cup) pecan nuts
6 spring onions, trimmed
55 g (2 oz/⅓ cup) dried cherries, cranberries or raisins
2 tablespoons chopped fresh coriander
1 tablespoon chopped fresh parsley
DRESSING:
100 ml (3½ fl oz/⅓ cup) olive oil
2 teaspoons raspberry vinegar
¼ teaspoon clear honey or sugar
salt and pepper

Cook the wild rice in a pan of lightly salted boiling water for 35-40 minutes until just tender. Cook the brown rice in a pan of lightly salted boiling water for 25 minutes or until just tender. Drain well and place both rices in a large bowl. Meanwhile, preheat oven to 220C (400F/Gas 6).

Roast the nuts in the oven for 5-6 minutes until browned; cool and coarsely chop. Set aside. Chop the spring onions and add to the rice with the dried fruit and herbs and stir well. Blend the dressing ingredients well together and pour over the salad, stir once, cover and leave rice to cool. Just before serving, toss in the roasted nuts and season to taste.

Serves 4-6.

—— BEETROOT & BEAN SALAD ——

25 g (1 oz/¼ cup) hazelnuts
450 g (1 lb) cooked beetroot, skinned
115 g (4 oz) green beans, trimmed
2 small leeks, trimmed
1 pear
115 g (4 oz/1 cup) cooked flageolet or haricot beans
DRESSING:
2 tablespoons chopped fresh dill
1 clove garlic, crushed
1 teaspoon wholegrain mustard
1 teaspoon sherry vinegar
85 ml (3 fl oz/⅓ cup) olive oil

Preheat oven to 200C (400F/Gas 6) and roast the hazelnuts for 6-8 minutes until golden. Cool slightly, chop and set aside. Cut the beetroot into bite-size pieces and place in a large bowl. Blanch the beans in boiling water for 1-2 minutes until tender. Drain, refresh under cold water and pat dry. Wash and thinly slice the leeks, then quarter, core and slice the pear. Add to the beetroot with the green beans and flageolet or haricot beans.

Mix the dill, garlic, mustard and vinegar together and whisk in the oil. Pour over the salad, toss well and set aside for 1 hour for the flavours to mingle. Sprinkle over the nuts and serve at once.

Serves 4-6.

Note: Use canned flageolet or haricot beans and drain well before use. Replace flageolet with cannellini beans, if preferred.

MEDITERRANEAN POTATO SALAD

450 g (1 lb) new potatoes
115 g (4 oz) French beans, trimmed
115 g (4 oz) trimmed fennel
25 g (1 oz/¼ cup) stoned olives
2 tablespoons capers, drained
2 tablespoons chopped fresh chives
2 teaspoons chopped fresh tarragon
55 ml (2 fl oz/¼ cup) virgin olive oil
juice ½ lemon
2 eggs
400 g (14 oz) can artichoke hearts, drained and halved

Cook the potatoes in a pan of lightly salted boiling water for 10-12 minutes until just cooked. Drain and place in a large bowl. Blanch the beans in boiling water for 1-2 minutes until just tender, drain and refresh under cold water; pat dry. Very thinly slice the fennel and halve the olives. Add to the potatoes with the beans, capers and herbs. Stir in the oil and lemon juice and set aside until potatoes are cold.

Hard-boil the eggs, plunge into cold water and peel. Roughly chop and add to the salad with the artichoke hearts. Toss well and serve at once.

Serves 4-6.

PANZANELLA SALAD

8 thick slices day-old Italian bread
10 plum tomatoes
½ small cucumber
½ small red onion
55 g (2 oz/½ cup) stoned black olives
2 tablespoons chopped fresh basil
grated zest 1 lemon
55 ml (2 fl oz/¼ cup) virgin olive oil
2 teaspoons balsamic vinegar
salt and pepper
lemon slices and basil sprigs, to garnish

Cut the bread into small cubes, place in a shallow dish and pour over enough water to lightly moisten. Set aside for 30 minutes.

Squeeze out all the excess water and crumble bread into a large bowl. Chop the tomatoes, cucumber, onion and olives into dice and add to the bread, with the basil and lemon zest. Stir well.

Whisk the oil and vinegar together, pour over the salad. Season and toss well until evenly combined. Cover and chill for at least 30 minutes, allowing the salad to return to room temperature before serving, garnished with lemon slices and basil sprigs.

Serves 4-6.

AUBERGINE SALAD

1 small aubergine (eggplant)
3 tablespoons olive oil
115 g (4 oz) shiitake mushrooms, wiped
450 g (1 lb) mixed salad leaves
1½ tablespoons chopped fresh coriander
25 g (1 oz/¼ cup) hazelnuts, toasted and coarsely
  chopped
DRESSING:
85 ml (3 fl oz/⅓ cup) olive oil
1 teaspoon sesame oil
2 teaspoons light soy sauce
1 tablespoon balsamic vinegar
½ teaspoon sugar
pepper

Preheat grill. Cut the aubergine (eggplant) into thin slices, brush with oil and grill for 2-3 minutes on each side, until charred and softened. Allow to cool. Thinly slice the mushrooms. Heat the remaining oil in a small frying pan and stir-fry the mushrooms over a medium heat for 3-4 minutes until tender. Drain on absorbent kitchen paper and leave to cool.

Wash the salad leaves, shake off all the excess water and place in a large bowl. Sprinkle over the coriander and nuts. Blend all the dressing ingredients together until well mixed. Add the aubergine (eggplant) and mushrooms to the salad, pour over the dressing, toss well and serve at once.

Serves 4.

—— TOMATO & PEACH SALAD ——

15 g (½ oz/¼ cup) basil leaves, coarsely chopped
1 clove garlic, chopped
15 g (½ oz/3 teaspoons) pine nuts, toasted
3 tablespoons virgin olive oil
1 tablespoon freshly grated Parmesan or vegetarian
  Cheddar cheese
115 ml (4 fl oz/½ cup) reduced-calorie mayonnaise
salt and pepper
2 large beef tomatoes
2 large ripe peaches
½ small red onion (optional)
grated zest 1 lemon
basil leaves, to garnish

Put the basil, garlic and pine nuts into a spice
grinder or food processor and purée until
fairly smooth. Blend in 2 tablespoons oil and
transfer to a small bowl. Stir in the cheese,
mayonnaise and salt and pepper. Cover and
chill until required.

Thinly slice the tomatoes. Stone the peaches
and cut into thin wedges; thinly slice the
onion, if using. Arrange the tomatoes and
peaches in rings on a large plate, sprinkle
over the onion and grated lemon zest. Spoon
the pesto dressing into the centre of the salad.
Drizzle the remaining tablespoon of oil over
the tomatoes and serve garnished with a few
basil leaves.

Serves 4.

PEA TABBOULEH

225 g (8 oz/1 ¼ cups) bulgar wheat
150 ml (5 fl oz/²⁄₃ cup) olive oil
1 clove garlic, crushed
1 tablespoon red wine vinegar
1 tablespoon chopped fresh coriander
1 tablespoon chopped fresh mint
1 teaspoon ground coriander
½ teaspoon ground cumin
115 g (4 oz) sugar snap peas, trimmed
115 g (4 oz/1 cup) frozen peas, thawed
1 large ripe peach, stoned and chopped
1 red onion, finely chopped
salt and pepper

Cover the bulgar wheat with plenty of cold water and leave to soak for 30 minutes. Drain well and squeeze out excess liquid. Mix together the oil, garlic, vinegar, herbs and spices and pour over the bulgar, stir well, cover and set aside for 30 minutes.

Cook the sugar snap peas in boiling water for 2 minutes and the peas for 1 minute. Drain both and refresh under cold water. Pat all the peas dry. Stir into the bulgar wheat with the peaches, onion and seasonings.

Serves 4-6.

WARM PASTA SALAD

225 g (8 oz) mixed mushrooms, wiped
25 g (1 oz/¼ cup) drained sun-dried tomatoes in oil,
  sliced
115 ml (4 fl oz/½ cup) olive oil
2 cloves garlic, chopped
grated zest 1 lemon
1 tablespoon lemon juice
2 tablespoons chopped fresh mint
225 g (8 oz/2½ cups) dried penne
2 ripe tomatoes, skinned, seeded and chopped
salt and pepper

Thinly slice the mushrooms and place in a large bowl with the sun-dried tomatoes.

Heat 1 tablespoon oil and sauté the garlic for 1 minute until starting to turn golden. Remove the pan from the heat and stir in the remaining oil, lemon zest, juice and mint, pour half over the mushrooms and reserve the rest. Stir mushrooms until well coated, cover and set aside to soften for several hours.

Cook the pasta in lightly salted, boiling water for 10 minutes until *al dente* (just cooked). Drain well, toss with the remaining dressing and stir into the marinated mushrooms with the fresh tomatoes. Season with salt and pepper.

Serves 4.

Note: Use a selection of button, field, oyster and shiitake mushrooms.

— SPINACH & CHEESE SALAD —

100 ml (3½ fl oz/⅓ cup) olive oil
3 shallots, thinly sliced
1 tablespoon red wine vinegar
1 tablespoon red wine
½ teaspoon sugar
225 g (8 oz) young spinach leaves
4 thick slices French bread
1 clove garlic, halved
115 g (4 oz) goat cheese, sliced
2 tablespoons pine nuts, toasted

Preheat oven to 190C (375F/Gas 5). In a small pan, heat 1 tablespoon oil and fry the shallots for 3-4 minutes until lightly golden.

Add the vinegar, wine and sugar and simmer gently for 5 minutes. Strain the juices into a bowl and reserve both the juices and the shallots. Wash the spinach leaves, shake off excess water, place in a plastic bag and chill for 1 hour to crisp. Meanwhile, place the sliced bread on a baking sheet and bake for 5 minutes. Rub the crisp sides all over with garlic, turn over and cook for a further 5 minutes to crisp the other sides. Rub these with garlic and return to the oven for a further 5-6 minutes until bread is completely crisp. Leave to cool.

Preheat grill. Place the spinach leaves in a bowl and toss in the shallots. Whisk the remaining oil into shallot juices and pour all but 1 tablespoon over the salad. Transfer to serving plates. Place a slice of cheese on top of each piece of bread and grill for 3-4 minutes until melted and browned. Place in the centre of each plate, pour the reserved dressing over the cheese and sprinkle over the pine nuts. Serve at once.

Serves 4.

- WATERCRESS & CHEESE SALAD -

85 g (3 oz/3 cups) watercress
85 g (3 oz/3 cups) rocket
1 ripe pear, quartered and sliced
15 g (½ oz/3 teaspoons) pumpkin seeds, toasted
85 g (3 oz) Gorgonzola cheese, crumbled
DRESSING:
3 tablespoons olive oil
½ teaspoon balsamic vinegar
1 teaspoon wholegrain mustard
1 tablespoon chopped fresh mint
salt and pepper

Trim and discard any thick stalks from the watercress. Wash and dry the watercress and rocket. Shake off excess water, transfer to a large bowl and stir in the sliced pear, pumpkin seeds and cheese.

Whisk all the dressing ingredients together until blended, pour over the salad, toss well and serve at once.

Serves 4.

NIÇOISE PLATTER

8 large asparagus spears, trimmed
115 g (4 oz) French beans, trimmed
175 g (6 oz) carrots, peeled
175 g (6 oz) peeled celeriac
115 g (4 oz) cooked beetroot, diced
430 g (15.2 oz) can haricot or navy beans
8 tablespoons olive oil
lemon juice
salt and pepper
1 clove garlic, crushed
1 teaspoon each red wine and raspberry vinegar
1 tablespoon chopped almonds, toasted
snipped chives and chopped fresh parsley
1 teaspoon wholegrain mustard
1 teaspoon creamed horseradish
8 marinated artichokes from a jar, halved

Peel almost to the tips of the asparagus and cook in boiling, salted water for 3 minutes until just tender. Drain, refresh and pat dry. Cook the beans for 2 minutes until tender; drain, refresh and pat dry. Finely grate the carrots and the celeriac; dice the beetroot. Drain, rinse and dry the haricot beans. Marinate the asparagus in 1 tablespoon oil, lemon juice and salt and pepper; set aside for 1 hour. Marinate the beans in a 1 tablespoon oil, garlic, red wine vinegar and salt and pepper; set aside for 1 hour.

Mix the grated carrot with 2 tablespoons oil, the raspberry vinegar, garlic, toasted almonds and chives. Mix the grated celeriac with 1 tablespoon oil, the mustard, lemon juice, salt and pepper. Mix the beetroot with the creamed horseradish and 1 tablespoon oil. Combine the haricot beans with 2 tablespoons olive oil, lemon juice, garlic, parsley and seasoning. Arrange all the vegetables on a large platter and serve.

Serves 8.

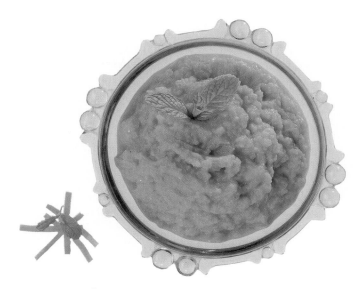

——— PURÉED GINGER CARROTS ———

900 g (2 lb) carrots, scrubbed
150 ml (5 fl oz/²⁄₃ cup) vegetable stock
2 tablespoons hazelnut oil
1 large onion, chopped
1 clove garlic, chopped
2 teaspoons grated fresh root ginger
1 teaspoon ground cumin
pinch of freshly grated nutmeg
salt and pepper
mint sprigs, to garnish

Roughly chop the carrots and place in a large pan with the stock. Bring slowly to the boil, cover and simmer gently for 20 minutes until carrots are cooked.

Heat 1 tablespoon oil and fry the onion, garlic, ginger and cumin for 5 minutes until soft. Transfer to a blender or food processor, add the cooked carrots and their juices and purée until smooth. Pass through a food mill or fine sieve if the purée is not completely smooth.

Beat in the remaining oil, freshly grated nutmeg and salt and pepper to taste and serve hot, garnished with mint.

Serves 6.

Note: This purée can easily be made ahead of time. To reheat, place in an ovenproof dish, cover with foil and bake in the oven for 20 minutes at 200C (400F/Gas 6). Or microwave on medium for 6-8 minutes until hot.

— CREAMY FENNEL & LEEK BAKE —

3 medium bulbs fennel, washed
2 leeks, trimmed and washed
400 ml (14 fl oz/1¾ cups) low-fat fromage frais
55 g (2 oz/½ cup) grated Cheddar cheese
¼ teaspoon freshly grated nutmeg
salt and pepper
1 clove garlic, halved
25 g (1 oz/¼ cup) freshly grated Parmesan cheese
25 g (1 oz/½ cup) fresh breadcrumbs
a little butter (optional)

Preheat oven to 200C (400F/Gas 6). Trim the fennel, discarding any discoloured outer leaves, and slice thinly. Reserve a few leaves for garnishing. Slice the fennel thinly.

Slice the leeks and place in a large bowl with the fennel. Stir in the fromage frais, Cheddar cheese, nutmeg and seasonings and stir well until evenly combined.

Rub the inside of a gratin or shallow baking dish with the garlic and spoon in the fennel mixture, smoothing the surface. Combine the Parmesan and breadcrumbs and sprinkle over the surface of the dish. Dot with a little butter, if wished. Cover loosely with foil and bake for 1 hour until fennel is tender. Remove foil and brown in the oven for a further 10 minutes, or under a preheated grill. Garnish with the reserved fennel and serve.

Serves 6-8.

— GARLIC-ROASTED POTATOES —

900 g (2 lb) new potatoes
12 unpeeled shallots
12 unpeeled cloves garlic
1 tablespoon chopped fresh sage
1 tablespoon chopped fresh thyme or rosemary
4 tablespoons hazelnut or olive oil
salt and pepper

Preheat oven to 200C (400F/Gas 6). Wash and dry the potatoes and halve any large ones. Trim the shallots, removing any dirt that may be trapped in the root ends and combine with the potatoes, garlic and herbs.

Put the oil into a roasting tin and place in the oven for 5 minutes until hot and starting to smoke. Add the potato and shallot mixture (taking care not to splash the hot oil) and stir until the potatoes, shallots, garlic and herbs are well coated.

Return to the oven and cook for 50-60 minutes until roasted and golden, turning from time to time to brown evenly. Transfer to a hot serving dish and serve at once.

Serves 6.

– BROCCOLI & CHILLI DRESSING –

900 g (2 lb) ripe tomatoes
3 tablespoons olive oil
1 clove garlic, crushed
2 teaspoons lemon juice
1 teaspoon hot chilli sauce
1 teaspoon balsamic vinegar
450 g (1 lb) broccoli
25 g (1 oz/¼ cup) stoned black olives, sliced
25 g (1 oz/¼ cup) pine nuts, toasted
1 tablespoon chopped fresh parsley
15 g (½ oz/¼ cup) Parmesan shavings

Place the tomatoes in a large heatproof bowl and pour over boiling water to cover.

Leave for 1 minute, then drain, refresh under cold water and pat dry. Skin and discard the skins and seeds and finely chop the flesh. Heat the oil in a large saucepan, add the tomatoes, garlic, lemon juice, chilli sauce and vinegar. Bring to the boil, cover and cook for 10 minutes. Uncover, increase the heat and cook until slightly reduced and thickened.

Meanwhile, trim the broccoli and steam for 5 minutes. Add to the sauce with the olives, nuts and parsley and stir well until combined. Transfer to a warmed serving dish, sprinkle over the Parmesan shavings and serve at once.

Serves 4.

Note: For vegans, omit the Parmesan cheese.

BEETROOT WITH HORSERADISH

six 150 g (5 oz) beetroot or 12-18 small beetroot
115 ml (4 fl oz/½ cup) natural yogurt
2 tablespoons mayonnaise
2 tablespoons chopped fresh chives
2 teaspoons grated horseradish (preferably fresh)
½ teaspoon wholegrain mustard
salt and pepper

Preheat oven to 180C (350F/Gas 4). Carefully wash the beetroot to remove any dirt, trim stalks to about 5 cm (2 in) and dry well.

Place in a small roasting pan, cover loosely with foil and bake for 2-2¼ hours until the skins wrinkle to the touch and the beetroot are tender.

Meanwhile, make the sauce. Mix all the remaining ingredients together in a small bowl and whisk until lightly thickened, adjust seasoning and chill for 2 hours. Cool the cooked beetroots for a few minutes and peel away the skins. Serve at once with the horseradish cream.

Serves 6.

—— SWEET POTATO 'CHIPS' ——

1-2 tablespoons olive oil
4 small sweet potatoes (about 700 g/1 ½ lb)
2 teaspoons paprika
½ teaspoon chilli powder
salt and pepper

Preheat oven to 230C (450F/Gas 8) and pour enough olive oil into a large roasting pan to just cover the base. Place in the oven for 2-3 minutes until hot.

Wash and dry the potatoes and cut each one into 8 wedges and carefully spoon into the hot oil, avoiding splashing. Bake at the top of the oven for 10 minutes, then turn potatoes over and return to the oven for a further 10 minutes until golden on the outside and cooked through.

Mix the spices together. Using a slotted spoon, transfer the potatoes to a serving dish. Add the spices and salt and pepper and stir well to coat evenly. Serve hot.

Serves 6.

Note: Reduce the quantity of oil, if wished.

SAUCY BEANS

175 g (6 oz/1 cup) dried butter or pinto beans, soaked
   overnight in cold water to cover
1 bay leaf
4 tablespoons virgin olive oil
1 red onion, chopped
2 cloves garlic, chopped
1 tablespoon chopped fresh sage
450 g (1 lb) ripe tomatoes
1 teaspoon balsamic vinegar
salt and pepper
1 tablespoon chopped fresh parsley

Drain the beans. Place in a pan with the bay
leaf and fresh water to cover. Bring to the
boil, then simmer, covered, for 40-45 minutes.

In a large pan, heat the oil and fry the onion,
garlic and sage for 10 minutes until golden.
Skin and deseed the tomatoes, chop flesh and
add to the pan with the vinegar. Cover and
cook for 5 minutes until softened.

Drain the cooked beans, rinse well and shake
off excess water. Stir into the onion mixture
in pan, cover and cook for 4-5 minutes until
heated through. Season to taste and sprinkle
over the chopped parsley. Serve with extra
olive oil drizzled over the beans.

Serves 4.

Note: This dish is delicious served warm or
cold. Pass round plenty of crusty bread to mop
up the juices.

- CHILLED SUMMER VEGETABLES -

225 g (8 oz) baby new potatoes, scrubbed
1 small fennel bulb, trimmed
115 g (4 oz) baby carrots
55 g (2 oz) baby sweetcorn
55 g (2 oz) asparagus tips
2 baby leeks, trimmed
4 spring onions, trimmed
2 tablespoons olive oil
250 ml (9 fl oz/1 cup) vegetable stock
grated zest and juice 1 lime
1/2 teaspoon coriander seeds, brusied
2 bay leaves
2 sprigs each parsley and coriander
2 tablespoons each sherry and wine vinegar
1 1/2 teaspoons caster sugar
4 ripe tomatoes, cut into wedges

Cook the potatoes in boiling water for 5 minutes, drain and set aside. Thickly slice the fennel, trim the carrots, sweetcorn and asparagus. Thickly slice the leeks and onions. Heat the oil in a large pan, add the fennel, carrots and sweetcorn and fry over a low heat for 5 minutes, add the asparagus, leeks, onions and potatoes and fry for 2 minutes. Add all the remaining ingredients to the pan, except the tomatoes, bring to the boil, cover and simmer gently for 6-8 minutes until all the vegetables are just cooked.

Strain the stock into a clean pan and transfer the vegetables to a large dish. Bring stock to the boil, stir in the tomatoes and simmer gently for 3 minutes. Pour mixture over the vegetables and leave to cool, then chill for several hours or overnight. Allow to return to room temperature and discard the herbs before serving.

Serves 4.

Note: Garnish with fresh herbs, if wished.

RICE WITH ASPARAGUS & NUTS

55 g (2 oz/¼ cup) butter
1 small onion, finely chopped
1 clove garlic, crushed
225 g (8 oz/1¼ cups) long-grain rice, washed well in
 cold water
450 ml (16 fl oz/2 cups) vegetable stock
225 g (8 oz) asparagus spears, trimmed
45 g (1½ oz/9 teaspoons) pine nuts
2 tablespoons chopped fresh sage
salt and pepper

Heat 15 g (½ oz/3 teaspoons) of the butter in a saucepan and fry the onion and garlic for 5 minutes. Add rice and stir-fry for 1 minute until transparent and glossy and pour in the stock. Bring to the boil, stir once, cover and cook gently for 12 minutes.

Steam the asparagus for 3 minutes, refresh under cold water, drain and dry well and coarsely chop. Heat the remaining butter in a large pan and stir-fry the pine nuts over a medium heat for 3-4 minutes until golden. Add the sage and asparagus and stir in the cooked rice. Season and heat through, stirring, for 2 minutes and serve at once.

Serves 6.

Note: For vegans, replace butter with 4 tablespoons olive oil.

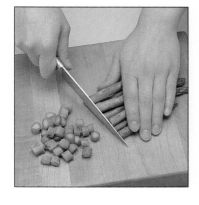

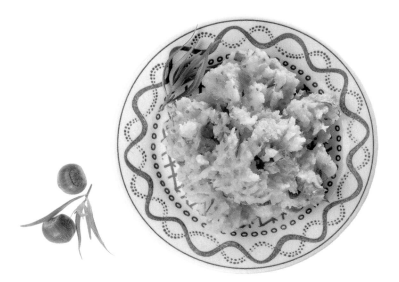

MASHED ARTICHOKES

350 g (12 oz) Jerusalem artichokes, scrubbed
225 g (8 oz) potatoes, scrubbed
2 tablespoons hazelnut oil
1 tablespoon chopped fresh tarragon
2 teaspoons wholegrain mustard
salt and pepper

Preheat oven to 200C (400F/Gas 6). Cut away any knobbly bits from the artichokes and cut any large ones in half.

Cut the potatoes into similar sized chunks and place both artichokes and potatoes in a roasting pan. Toss with 1 tablespoon of the oil and bake for 35-40 minutes until artichokes and potatoes are cooked.

Pass through a food mill or mash well and stir in the remaining oil, tarragon and mustard. Season to taste and serve hot.

Serves 4.

Note: Use sweet potatoes when Jerusalem artichokes are unavailable.

FRICASSÉE OF GREENS

1 tablespoon olive oil
1 leek, trimmed and sliced
115 g (4 oz) French beans, trimmed
115 g (4 oz) sugar snap peas, trimmed
3 tablespoons vegetable stock
½ teaspoon sugar
115 g (4 oz) mange tout (snow peas), trimmed
115 g (4 oz/1 cup) podded peas, thawed if frozen
grated zest and juice ½ lemon
1 tablespoon chopped fresh mint
1 tablespoon chopped fresh chives
15 g (½ oz/3 teaspoons) butter
salt and pepper

In a large pan, heat the oil and fry the leek for 2 minutes. Add the French beans and sugar snap peas and stir-fry for 1 minute. Add the stock and sugar, cover and simmer gently for 2 minutes.

Add the mange tout (snow peas) and peas to the pan, cover and cook for a further 2 minutes. Remove from the heat and stir in the lemon zest and juice, herbs, butter and salt and pepper and serve immediately.

Serves 4.

Note: For vegans, replace butter with 1 tablespoon olive oil.

CREAMED BEANS

700 g (1½ lb) podded broad beans, peeled and outer
    shells removed
2 tablespoons olive oil
1 leek, trimmed and thinly sliced
85 ml (3 fl oz/⅓ cup) vegetable stock
1 tablespoon chopped fresh parsley
2 teaspoons chopped fresh tarragon
75 g (3 oz/⅓ cup) low-fat cream cheese
15 g (½ oz/¼ cup) grated Parmesan or vegetarian
    Cheddar cheese
salt and pepper
toasted bread triangles, to serve
parsley sprigs, to garnish

Preheat oven to 200C (400F/Gas 6). Wash
the beans and pat dry. In a large pan, heat 1
tablespoon oil and fry the leek for 5 minutes
until soft, then add the beans and stir-fry for
2 minutes. Add the stock and simmer,
uncovered, for 3 minutes. Purée the beans in
a blender or food processor with the herbs and
cream cheese, salt and pepper until smooth.
Transfer to a shallow ovenproof dish and
level the surface.

Sprinkle over the Parmesan or Cheddar
cheese. Drizzle over the remaining olive oil
and bake for 10 minutes until bubbling.
Brown under a hot grill and arrange triangles
of toasted bread around the dish. Garnish
with parsley sprigs and serve hot.

Serves 6.

Note: If possible use fresh broad beans. You
will need approximately double the amount
of unpodded beans. Alternatively use frozen
beans and thaw before using.

—— BARLEY WITH VERMICELLI ——

55 g (2 oz/¼ cup) butter
1 red onion, thinly sliced
½ red pepper (capsicum), seeded and thinly sliced
2 large ripe tomatoes, skinned, seeded and diced
175 g (6 oz/⅔ cup) pearl barley
55 g (2 oz) dried vermicelli
1 tablespoon chopped fresh parsley
450 ml (16 fl oz/2 cups) vegetable stock
salt and pepper

Preheat oven to 200C (400F/Gas 6). Heat the butter in a large flameproof casserole dish and fry the onion and pepper (capsicum) for 3 minutes. Stir in the tomatoes and simmer for a further 2 minutes.

Wash the barley with cold water, drain throughly and stir into the pan. Add the vermicelli, breaking it into short lengths as you go, and stir-fry for 2 minutes. Add the parsley and stock, cover with foil and bake for 50-60 minutes until all the liquid is absorbed and the barley is tender. Season well and serve with a crisp green salad.

Serves 4.

Note: For vegans, replace butter with 3 tablespoons olive oil.

BUTTERY COUSCOUS

350 g (12 oz/2 cups) couscous
175 g (6 oz/1⅓ cups) podded broad beans
200 g (7 oz) can sweetcorn kernels, drained
115 g (4 oz/1 cup) podded peas
115 g (4 oz/½ cup) butter
1 teaspoon ground cumin
1 teaspoon ground paprika
1 tablespoon chopped fresh coriander
25 g (1 oz/¼ cup) chopped mixed nuts, toasted
juice ½ lime
salt and pepper

Wash the couscous until all the grains are moistened and set aside to soak for 5 minutes. Stir grains with a fork to separate and steam for 12-15 minutes until fluffed up and tender. Peel and discard the tough outer skins of the beans and blanch in boiling water for 2 minutes; drain and dry well. Blanch the sweetcorn for 2 minutes and the peas for 1 minute; drain and dry well.

In a large pan, heat the butter, stir in the spices and cook gently for 2 minutes. Add the blanched vegetables and fry for a further 2 minutes. Fork the cooked couscous to break up any lumps and stir into the pan until well coated with butter. Stir in the coriander, nuts, lime juice and season well. Serve hot.

Serves 4-6.

—CAULIFLOWER & COCONUT—

1 cauliflower
2 tablespoons light olive oil
1 teaspoon sesame oil
1 red chilli, seeded and sliced
1 cm (½ in) piece fresh root ginger, peeled and finely
   chopped
2 shallots, thinly sliced
25 g (1 oz/⅓ cup) desiccated coconut
1 tablespoon light soy sauce
1 teaspoon sherry vinegar

Trim and discard the cauliflower leaves and
cut out the central core. Cut flowerets into
bite-sized pieces and steam for 5-6 minutes
until just tender.

Meanwhile, heat 1 tablespoon olive oil and
the sesame oil in a non-stick frying pan and
fry the chilli, ginger and shallots for 5
minutes until softened.

Add the coconut and stir-fry over a medium
heat for 3-4 minutes until golden. Stir in the
cauliflower, remaining oil, soy sauce and
vinegar and serve hot or warm.

Serves 4.

HERBED LENTILS

225 g (8 oz/1¼ cups) Puy (or continental) lentils,
  soaked overnight in cold water to cover
85 ml (3 fl oz/⅓ cup) olive oil
2 shallots, finely chopped
2 cloves garlic, crushed
1½ tablespoons chopped fresh mint
1½ tablespoons chopped fresh tarragon
1 tablespoon balsamic vinegar
salt and pepper

Drain the soaked lentils and place in a large saucepan. Cover with fresh cold water, bring to the boil, cover and simmer for 35-40 minutes until lentils are tender. Drain well.

In a large pan, heat the oil and fry the shallots and garlic for 5 minutes. Stir in the mint, tarragon, lentils and vinegar and cook gently for 5 minutes. Season to taste and serve hot or cold.

Serves 6-8.

Note: Puy or continental lentils have a particularly nutty flavour but green lentils can be used instead, if wished.

——MUSHROOM RATATOUILLE——

15 g (½ oz/¼ cup) dried ceps (mushrooms)
150 ml (5 fl oz/⅔ cup) boiling water
400 g (14 oz) can chopped tomatoes
3 tablespoons olive oil
1 clove garlic, crushed
1 tablespoon chopped fresh basil
1 large onion, chopped
2 teaspoons chopped fresh thyme
525 g (1 lb 2 oz) mixed mushrooms, wiped
salt and pepper

Place the ceps in a small bowl and pour over the boiling water. Set aside for 20 minutes to soak. Strain, reserving the liquid, and chop the ceps and reserve.

Place the tomatoes, 1 tablespoon oil, garlic and basil in a pan. Bring to the boil and simmer for 20 minutes.

Heat the remaining oil in a large frying pan and fry the onion and thyme for 5 minutes. Add the ceps and fresh mushrooms and stir-fry over a high heat for 3-4 minutes until golden. Add the cep liquid and simmer for 3 minutes, stir in the tomato sauce and simmer gently for a further 5 minutes. Season and serve hot, warm or cold with crisp French bread.

Serves 4-6.

— MOCHA ESPRESSO ICE CREAM —

450 ml (16 fl oz/2 cups) milk
150 ml (5 fl oz/⅔ cup) double (thick) cream
25 g (1 oz/⅓ cup) medium ground espresso coffee
85 g (3 oz) plain (dark) chocolate, chopped
6 egg yolks
175 g (6 oz/¾ cup) caster sugar
chocolate shavings, to decorate

Place the milk, cream, coffee grains and 55 g (2 oz) of the chocolate in a small saucepan and heat slowly until almost boiling. Remove from the heat and set aside for 30 minutes for the flavours to infuse.

Beat the egg yolks and sugar together in a large bowl until thick and pale. Gradually beat in the mocha mixture and transfer to a clean saucepan. Heat gently, stirring, until the mixture thickens, but do not allow to boil. Leave to cool.

Transfer the mixture to a plastic container and freeze. Beat to mix and break up ice crystals after about 1 hour and again at hourly intervals until almost firm. Stir in the remaining chocolate, cover and allow to freeze completely. Remove from the freezer for 20 minutes before serving to allow ice cream to soften. Decorate with chocolate shavings, if wished.

Serves 4.

– WHOLEWHEAT NUT BISCOTTI –

2 eggs
100 g (3½ oz/⅓ cup) caster sugar
225 g (8 oz/1¾ cups) wholewheat flour
1½ teaspoons baking powder
pinch of salt
1 tablespoon light olive oil
115 g (4 oz/¾ cup) Brazil nuts, toasted and ground
½ teaspoon caraway seeds
½ teaspoon freshly grated lemon zest

Preheat oven to 180C (350F/Gas 4) and lightly oil a baking sheet. Beat the eggs and sugar together until very thick and pale.

Beat in the flour, baking powder and salt to form a soft, sticky dough. Stir in the remaining ingredients and turn out onto a clean surface. Divide dough in half and roll into 2 logs about 5 x 20 cm (2 x 8 in) and transfer to the prepared baking sheet. Bake for 20 minutes. Remove from the oven and increase oven temperature to 200C (400F/Gas 6).

Using a serrated knife, cut the logs into 1 cm (½ in) biscuits, slicing diagonally. Place biscuits, cut-sides down, on the baking sheet and return to the oven for 8-10 minutes until browned around the edges. Cool on a wire tray.

Makes 32 biscuits.

Note: Sprinkle the biscuits with a little icing sugar, if wished.

—LEMON POPPY SEED CAKE—

4 eggs, separated
115 g (4 oz/½ cup) caster sugar
freshly grated zest and juice 1 lemon
85 g (3 oz/¾ cup) ground almonds
85 g (3 oz/¾ cup) dried breadcrumbs
15 g (½ oz/3 teaspoons) poppy seeds
2 tablespoons brandy
RASPBERRY SAUCE:
225 g (8 oz) fresh raspberries
1 tablespoon clear honey
½ teaspoon ground cinnamon

Preheat oven to 180C (350F/Gas 4) and grease and base-line a 20 cm (8 in) spring-release tin. Beat the egg yolks, sugar and lemon zest and juice together until pale and creamy. Whisk the egg whites until stiff. Fold in with the almonds, breadcrumbs and poppy seeds until evenly combined. Transfer to the prepared tin and bake for 40 minutes until golden and firm to the touch. Remove from the oven and spike all over with a cocktail stick. Pour over the brandy and leave to cool.

Make the sauce. Reserve 12 raspberries for decoration and purée the rest in a blender or food processor until smooth. Pass through a fine sieve to remove the pips and whisk in the honey and cinnamon. Serve the cake cut into wedges, topped with the reserved raspberries and the sauce.

Serves 6.

Note: Frozen raspberries can be substituted for fresh, if more convenient.

-FIGS WITH CINNAMON CREAM-

9 large ripe figs
55 g (2 oz/¼ cup) unsalted butter
4 teaspoons brandy
15 g (½ oz/3 teaspoons) brown sugar
almond flakes, to decorate
CINNAMON CREAM:
150 ml (5 fl oz/⅔ cup) double (thick) cream
1 teaspoon ground cinnamon
1 tablespoon brandy
2 teaspoons clear honey

Prepare the cinnamon cream. Combine all the ingredients in a small bowl, cover and refrigerate for 30 minutes to allow time for flavours to develop.

Preheat grill. Halve the figs and thread onto 6 skewers. Melt the butter in a small pan and stir in the brandy.

Brush the figs with the brandy butter and sprinkle with a little sugar. Place under a hot grill for 4-5 minutes until bubbling and golden. Whip the cinnamon cream until just holding its shape, decorate with almond flakes, and serve with the grilled figs.

Serves 6.

PEARS WITH CHOCOLATE SAUCE

115 g (4 oz/½ cup) ricotta cheese
55 g (2 oz/½ cup) ground hazelnuts
2 tablespoons clear honey
2 small egg yolks
seeds from 1 cardamom pod, crushed
4 large pears
CHOCOLATE SAUCE:
115 g (4 oz) plain chocolate
45 g (1½ oz/9 teaspoons) unsalted butter
2 tablespoons brandy
2 tablespoons thick sour cream

Cream together the ricotta cheese, hazelnuts, honey, egg yolks and crushed cardamom seeds.

Preheat oven to 190C (375F/Gas 5). Cut a thin slice from the base of each pear and using a corer or small spoon, carefully scoop out the core as far up inside the pear as possible, without damaging the flesh. Fill cavities with the ricotta mixture, pressing in well; smooth the bases flat. Peel the pears and place in a small roasting tin. Cover with foil and bake for 45-50 minutes until pears are cooked.

Just before pears are cooked, place the chocolate, butter, brandy and thick sour cream in a small pan and heat gently until melted, stir well and keep warm. Transfer the cooked pears to serving plates, slice in half to reveal filling and pour over the sauce. Serve immediately.

Serves 4.

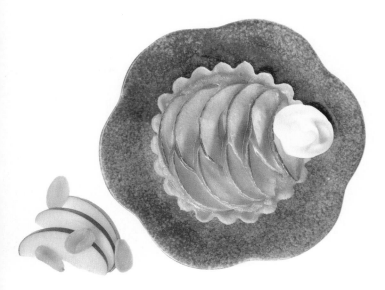

—APPLE & ALMOND TARTLETS—

350 g (12 oz) prepared shortcrust pastry
85 g (3 oz/⅓ cup) unsalted butter, softened
85 g (3 oz/⅓ cup) caster sugar
2 eggs, beaten
55 g (2 oz/½ cup) ground almonds
1 teaspoon ground cinnamon
85 g (3 oz) vegetarian Cheshire or Cheddar cheese
3 small dessert apples
2 tablespoons apricot jam

Divide the pastry into 6 portions. Roll out each portion and use to line six 10 cm (4 in) tartlet tins. Prick the bases and chill for 30 minutes.

Preheat oven to 190C (375F/Gas 5) and place a baking sheet on the middle shelf. Cream the butter and sugar together until soft and beat in the eggs, almonds and cinnamon. Finely grate the cheese and stir into the mixture. Line pastry cases with foil and baking beans and bake blind on the heated baking sheet for 10 minutes. Remove the beans and foil and bake for a further 8-10 minutes until pastry is crisp and golden. Cool slightly and spread the cheese mixture over the bases.

Quarter and core the apples and cut into thin slices. Arrange the slices over the cheese mixture in circles and bake for 15 minutes. Reduce the oven temperature to 180C (350F/Gas 4) and cook for a further 10-15 minutes until firm to the touch. Heat the jam with 1 teaspoon of water until melted, pass through a fine sieve and carefully brush over the tartlets to glaze. Serve warm with a spoonful of crème fraîche or fromage frais.

Serves 6.

— BAKED MANGO CUSTARDS —

2 large ripe mangoes
juice 1 lime
4 egg yolks
85 g (3 oz/¹⁄₃ cup) caster sugar
1 teaspoon ground ginger
¹⁄₄ teaspoon ground mixed spice
550 ml (20 fl oz/2¹⁄₂ cups) double (thick) cream
toasted flaked almonds, to decorate

Preheat oven to 160C (325F/Gas 3). Peel the mangoes, cut away and discard the stone and coarsely chop the flesh. Place in a blender or food processor, add the lime juice and purée until smooth.

Beat the egg yolks, sugar and spices together until pale and thick and stir in the mango purée. Put 450 ml (16 fl oz/2 cups) double (thick) cream into a pan and heat until gently simmering. Beat into the mango mixture until evenly blended and pour into 8 ramekin dishes. Place in a roasting pan and pour in enough boiling water to come two-thirds of the way up the sides of the dishes. Bake for 30 minutes, remove from the oven and leave to cool, then chill for several hours.

Beat the remaining cream until stiff and spoon or pipe a swirl onto each custard and decorate with the almonds.

Makes 8.

EXOTIC FRUIT BRÛLÉE

3 egg yolks
55 g (2 oz/¼ cup) vanilla sugar
150 ml (5 fl oz/⅔ cup) crème fraîche
2 teaspoons kirsch or brandy
1 small ripe mango, peeled
1 small ripe pear, peeled, quartered and cored
1 large ripe fig
8 large ripe strawberries, hulled
freshly grated nutmeg
tuille biscuits, to serve

Preheat grill. Beat the egg yolks and sugar together until pale and thick and stir in the crème fraîche and kirsch or brandy; set aside. Remove the mango stone and cut the flesh into thin slices; slice the pear, fig and strawberries thinly. Arrange all the fruit over the bases of 4 individual gratin dishes or flame-proof plates.

Carefully pour a quarter of the sauce over each dish, as evenly as possible, to cover the fruit and grate over a little fresh nutmeg. Place under a medium grill and cook for 3-4 minutes until the sauce is lightly caramelised. Cool slightly and serve with tuille or other sweet biscuits.

Serves 4.

— MELON & CHILLED BERRIES —

350 g (12 oz) mixed fresh berries (raspberries,
 strawberries, blackberries, blueberries)
115 ml (4 fl oz/½ cup) Muscat dessert wine
1 teaspoon chopped preserved stem ginger
2 teaspoons stem ginger syrup (from jar)
1 teaspoon shredded fresh mint
2 small Cantaloupe or Charentais melons
mint leaves, to decorate

Wash and dry the berries and hull and halve
as necessary. Place in a bowl and pour over
the wine, ginger, ginger syrup and mint. Stir
well, cover and chill for 2 hours.

With a sharp knife, cut the melons in half,
cutting into the flesh in a zig-zag pattern all
the way around the centre of each fruit to
form attractive edges. Carefully scoop out
and discard the seeds and fill each hollow
with a large spoonful of the chilled berries.
Pour in the juices, decorate with mint leaves
and serve with crème fraîche or mascarpone
cheese.

Serves 4.

-FRUIT & ELDERFLOWER CREAM -

115 ml (4 fl oz/½ cup) double (thick) cream
115 ml (4 fl oz/½ cup) fromage frais
2 tablespoons elderflower syrup
1 small ripe mango
1 small ripe papaya
1 large ripe peach
1 large apple
115 g (4 oz) strawberries
115 g (4 oz) bunch seedless grapes
freshly grated nutmeg and fresh lemon balm or mint,
    to decorate

Whip the double (thick) cream and gently fold in the fromage frais and elderflower syrup, cover and chill until required.

Peel the mango, cut down either side of the stone and cut the flesh into thin slices. Peel and halve the papaya, scoop out and discard the seeds and cut flesh into thin strips. Halve and stone the peach and cut into thin wedges. Quarter and core the apple and cut into thin wedges. Hull and halve the strawberries.

Arrange all the prepared fruit and the grapes on a large platter and place the bowl of elderflower dip in the centre. Sprinkle over a little nutmeg and serve the fruit decorated with the lemon balm or mint.

Serves 8.

Note: Use any fruit liqueur such as crème de cassis or crème de peche as an alternative to elderflower syrup, if wished. Sprinkle lemon juice over the fruit if not serving immediately.

INDEX